Party Animal Cakes

Lindy Smith

15 fantastic designs plus quick cup cakes and cookies for extra bite!

D&C
David and Charles

A DAVID & CHARLES BOOK
Copyright © David & Charles Limited 2006

David & Charles is an F+W Publications Inc. company
4700 East Galbraith Road
Cincinnati, OH 45236

First published in the UK in 2006

Text and project designs copyright © Lindy Smith 2006

Lindy Smith has asserted her right to be identified as author of this work in accordance with
the Copyright, Designs and Patents Act, 1988.

A catalogue record for this book is available from the British Library.

ISBN-13: 978-0-7153-2208-6 hardback
ISBN-10: 0-7153-2208-7 hardback

ISBN-13: 978-0-7153-2207-9 paperback
ISBN-10: 0-7153-2207-9 paperback

Printed in China by SNP Leefung
for David & Charles
Brunel House Newton Abbot Devon

Commissioning Editor Fiona Eaton
Editor Jennifer Proverbs
Art Editor Lisa Wyman
Designers Louise Prentice and Sarah Clark
Production Controller Kelly Smith
Project Editor Jan Cutler
Photographer Karl Adamson

Visit our website at www.davidandcharles.co.uk

David & Charles books are available from all good bookshops; alternatively you can contact
our Orderline on 0870 9908222 or write to us at FREEPOST EX2 110, D&C Direct, Newton
Abbot, TQ12 4ZZ (no stamp required UK only); US customers call 800-289-0963 and
Canadian customers call 800-840-5220.

Contents

Introduction

This is a cake book that I've always wanted to write, as the topic particularly appeals to me. The research has been fun, especially the necessary visits with my children to London Zoo and to local and national natural history museums. Of course, animals living freely in reserves throughout the world are a regular feature on our television screens and these have also given me inspiration. The animal world is full of surprises, and however much you know there is always more to discover. Did you know, for example, that the largest tigers live in Siberia, and a male African elephant can grow to almost 4m (13ft) tall?

The first novelty cake I ever made was a large pink pig for my daughter Charlotte's second birthday; it didn't exactly turn out as I'd hoped, at that stage I still had a lot to learn, but she was thrilled. My children, like many others, are fascinated by the natural world, so over the years I've had requests to make all kinds of animals, from sharks and sailfishes to squirrels and butterflies. I enjoy creating these cakes immensely, as they almost seem to come alive and develop characters of their own while being made. Also, like us, animals are not 100 per cent symmetrical, so it doesn't matter if one ear is larger than another or if an eye is slightly lopsided – in fact it can add to the appeal of the cake!

Have fun and enjoy,

Lindy

lindy@lindyscakes.co.uk
www.lindyscakes.co.uk

About this book

Included are cakes that will appeal to all ages: a spiky hedgehog covered in chocolate spines, a Hallowe'en bat with opened wings, a water-spouting whale, an elegant cat wearing a diamanté-effect collar, and a lively farmyard birthday party for pigs, complete with food, streamers, party hats and balloons. You will find everything you need to create the delightful animal cakes, including a range of clearly explained standard sugarcraft techniques as well as some new ones to add to your repertoire. To make the cakes realistic and fun, each is carved to shape, and to ensure success with this you will find detailed carving instructions, templates and sketches. All the recipes you will need are included, as well as cup cake and cookie recipes. Among the techniques are instructions for making moulds so that you can produce a series of identical models to decorate cup cakes for a particular theme. Instructions on growing sugar crystals are also given – a fun and delightful idea for making jewel-like cake decorations.

Most of the cakes are covered in sugarpaste (rolled fondant), which always gives a smooth covering that can be blended around curved shapes. For those who prefer buttercream as a cake covering you will find a splendid sheep cake decorated entirely in buttercream, introducing another technique for you to try: layers of buttercream whirls to suggest a curly fleece.

Also offered are dainty bitesize and mini-cakes that have been decorated to match the main cake. They make ideal gifts, and children love to get involved with making them, too. Other main cakes are accompanied by matching cup cakes or cookies, giving you plenty of scope for creativity and improvization.

How to use this book

Please read the reference section at the front of the book thoroughly; it explains how to begin tackling the cakes as well as some basic techniques. The projects use a variety of implements, and the most frequently used are listed in the Equipment List on pages 6–7. Where particular makes of cutters or decorations are specified in the materials lists you will find an abbreviation for the name of the supplier in brackets. Please refer to the abbreviations list at the beginning of Suppliers on page 104.

Recipes for the cakes, including baking times and quantities for various shapes, as well as all the different types of icing used in the book, are provided. To help you create the cakes, half-size templates are provided at the back of the book for projects where you will need to cut out a complicated shape. You will also find carving sketches for cakes that need to be intricately carved.

For a professional look you will need to use paste colours and dusts, and there are some good-quality decorations that you may wish to use to enhance your creation. These can be obtained from cake-decorating stores or by mail order; suppliers of sugarcraft equipment and ingredients can be found at the back of the book.

Tackling Cakes

Although you will be keen to get started on one of the fantastic cake projects in this book, take a little time to read this section so that you are familiar with some important and basic points. This will help you to achieve the best results.

Preparation

If your cake is to be a creation that you will be proud of, you will need to be fully prepared. Before you start your chosen project, read through the instructions carefully so that you understand what is involved and how much time to allow. Make sure you have all the materials and items of equipment to hand to complete the project.

Time planning

Try not to leave everything to the last minute, and plan your decorating time in advance. As the cakes baked from the recipes in this book last about two weeks, you have about one week to decorate the cake, leaving a week for it to be eaten.

Each project is split into stages to indicate natural breaks in the decorating process; for example, a simple two-stage project, such as Cheeky Chimp, could be carved and decorated over a two-day period. Some projects are obviously more involved than others; for example, Farmyard Feast and Take It Easy, so try to be realistic with what time you have available, and plan well in advance.

Cheeky Chimp can be made over two days.

Lining tins

It is quite simple to line tins (pans) well. Neatly lined tins will prevent the cake mixture from sticking and help to ensure a good shape.

1 Measure the circumference of your tin and cut a strip of baking parchment slightly longer to allow for an overlap. Make the strip 5cm (2in) deeper than the height of the tin. Fold up 2.5cm (1in) along the bottom of the strip. For a round or heart-shaped tin cut this fold with diagonal cuts. For a square, rectangular or hexagonal tin, crease the strip at intervals equal to the length of the inside edges of the tin, and then cut the folded section where it is creased into mitres (**A**).

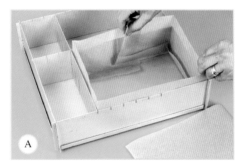

2 Grease the tin and place the strip around the side(s) with the cut edge on the base. Position baking parchment to fit the base (**B**).

3 Care needs to be taken when lining ball tins. Cut two circles of the appropriate size from baking paper:

✿ 15cm (6in) for a 10cm (4in) ball
✿ 20cm (8in) for a 12.5cm (4⅞in) ball
✿ 25.5cm (10in) for a 15cm (6in) ball

4 Fold the circles into quarters to find their centres. Open out the circles and make radial cuts into the circle (**C**). Grease both the tin and one side of the paper and place the circle into the centre of one half of the tin, greased sides together. Encourage the paper to fit the tin by overlapping the sections.

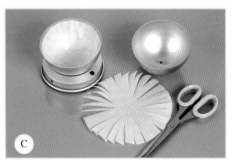

Equipment List

Cocktail sticks Used as markers and to transfer small amounts of paste colour (1).

Craft knife for intricate cutting tasks (2).

Cutters:
✿ Blossom plunger set (PME) used on Flower Power (3).

✿ Circle, plastic, and small and large metal (4).

✿ Elegant Heart (LC) used on Pool Party, Purrfectly Exotic and Squeak with Delight (5).

✿ Heart (6)

✿ Large Blossom (FMM) used on Flower Power (7).

✿ Ovals plastic and small metal (FMM) for cutting out eyes and fish scales (8).

✿ Paisley (LC) used on Purrfectly Exotic and Tall Story (9).

✿ Stars (LC) used on Vamp It Up! (10).

Dowel used to create stable cakes and for making holes (11).

Embossers:
✿ Pan scourers (12).

✿ Trellis (PC) (13).

Foam for supporting paste during drying (14).

Measuring spoons for accurate measuring of ingredients (15).

Multisized ribbon cutter (FMM) time-saving tool for cutting even strips of paste (16).

Paintbrushes including stippling brush. A range of sizes is useful for painting and dusting (17).

Paint palette for mixing paste colours (18).

Palette knife for cutting paste (19).

Pins (glass-headed, dressmakers') used to hold templates temporarily in position (20).

Piping bag and coupler to hold buttercream or royal icing while piping. The coupler is connected to the piping bag and allows the tube to be changed easily (21).

Piping tubes (tips) for piping buttercream, royal icing and softened modelling paste, and for cutting out small circles (22).

Posy pick for inserting into cakes to hold wires (23).

Rolling pins for rolling out all the different types of paste (24).

Scissors for cutting templates and trimming paste to shape (25).

Smoother helps to create a smooth and even finish to sugarpaste (rolled fondant) (26).

Spacers (narrow and 5mm ($^{3}/_{16}$in)) for rolling out an even thickness of paste (27).

Sugar shaper with discs creates pieces of uniformly shaped modelling paste (28).

Tins (pans) medium ball, multisized and multi-round for baking cakes (29).

Tools:
✿ Ball tool, makes even indentations in paste and is used to curve small pieces of paste (30).

✿ Cutting wheel used instead of a knife to avoid dragging the paste (31).

✿ Dresden tool, to create markings on paste (32).

✿ Scriber for scribing around templates (33).

Work board, non-stick used for rolling out pastes (34).

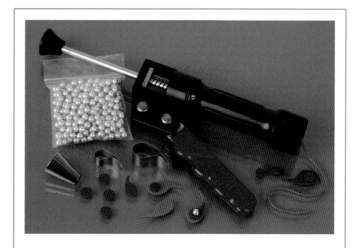

Using the correct equipment will ensure professional results quickly and simply.

Piping tubes

The following piping tubes (tips) have been used in the book. As tube numbers may vary with different suppliers, always check the tube diameter:

Tube No.	Diameter
1	1mm (⅟₃₂in)
1.5	1.2mm (⅟₃₂in)
2	1.5mm (⅟₁₆in)
4	3mm (⅛in)
16	5mm (³⁄₁₆in)
17	6mm (¼in)
18	7mm (⅝₂in)

Cup and US measurements

For readers who prefer to use cup measurements, please use the following conversions (note: 1 tbsp = 15ml; Australian tablespoons are 20ml):

butter 100g (3½oz) = 1 stick, 225g (8oz) = 1 cup, 25g (1oz) = 2 tbsp, 15g (½ oz) = 1 tbsp

caster (superfine) sugar 200g (7oz) = 1 cup, 25g (1oz) = 2 tbsp

desiccated (dry unsweetened shredded) coconut 75g (3oz) = 1 cup, 4 tbsp = 25g (1oz)

flour 150g (5oz) = 1 cup

glacé (candied) cherries 225g (8oz) = 1 cup

icing (confectioners') sugar 115g (4oz) = 1 cup

liquid 250ml (9fl oz) = 1 cup, 125ml (4fl oz) = ½ cup

soft brown sugar 115g (4oz) = 1 cup

sultanas 175g (6oz) = 1 cup

Baking Cakes

The projects in this book have been made using tried-and-tested recipes for Madeira and chocolate cake, which will give you perfect results. Both cakes are moist and light in texture but also firm enough to be carved to form the intricate shapes often used. A variety of flavourings can be used with the Madeira cake in place of the traditional lemon, and try to use the best-quality chocolate for the chocolate cake for a heavenly flavour.

Madeira cake

This is a firm, moist cake that will keep for up to two weeks. This allows one week to decorate the cake and one for it to be eaten. See the facing page for the quantities for each recipe.

1 Preheat the oven to 160°C/325°F/Gas 3. Grease and line the cake tin (pan) with baking parchment (see page 5).

2 Cream the butter and sugar in a large mixing bowl until light, fluffy and pale. Sift the flours together in a separate bowl.

3 Beat the eggs into the creamed mixture, one at a time, following each with a spoonful of flour, to prevent the mixture from curdling.

4 Sift the remaining flour into the creamed mixture and fold in carefully with a large metal spoon. Add the flavouring, if using.

5 Transfer to the lined bakeware. Please note that baking times will vary and depend on your oven, the cakes tin used and the depth of the cake. When the cake is ready it will be well risen, firm to the touch and a skewer inserted into the centre will come out clean.

6 Leave the cake to cool in the tin, then, leaving the lining paper on, wrap the cake in foil or place in an airtight container for at least 12 hours before cutting, to allow the cake to settle.

Make sure your eggs are at room temperature before you start baking.

Flavourings

Traditionally, Madeira cake was flavoured with lemon, but it can also be made with other flavourings (flavourings are given for a six-egg quantity Madeira cake; increase or decrease the amounts of flavourings for other quantities):

Lemon: grated rind of 2 lemons
Vanilla: 5ml (1 tsp) vanilla extract
Cherry: 350g (12oz) glacé (candied) cherries, halved
Fruit: 350g (12oz) sultanas (golden raisins), currants, raisins or chopped dates
Coconut: 110g (3¾oz) desiccated (dry unsweetened shredded) coconut
Almond: 5ml (1 tsp) almond extract and 45ml (3 tbsp) ground almonds

Chocolate cake

This is a rich, moist, yet firm, chocolate cake. The secret to success is to use good-quality chocolate with a reasonably high cocoa solids content; luxury plain Belgian chocolate with a cocoa solid content of around 50 per cent, for example, works well. See facing page for the quantities.

1 Preheat the oven to 180°C/350°F/Gas 4. Grease and line the cake tin (pan) with baking parchment (see page 5).

2 Melt the chocolate either in a heatproof bowl over a pan of simmering water or in a microwave. Cream the butter and sugar in a large mixing bowl until light, fluffy and pale.

3 Separate the eggs. Gradually add the egg yolks, then the melted chocolate. In a separate bowl, whisk the egg whites to soft peaks. Gradually whisk the icing sugar into the egg whites.

4 Sift the flour into another bowl and, using a large metal spoon, gently fold the flour alternately with the egg whites into the chocolate mixture.

5 Transfer the mixture into the lined bakeware and bake. Baking times will depend on your oven, the cake tin used and the depth of the cake. Check small cakes after 30 minutes, medium-sized cakes after an hour, and large cakes after 2 hours. When the cake is baked it will be well risen, firm to the touch and a skewer inserted into the centre will come out clean.

6 Leave the cake to cool completely in the tin, then, leaving the lining paper on, wrap the cake in foil or place in an airtight container for at least 12 hours before cutting, to allow the cake to settle.

Break each egg into a cup to prevent small pieces of eggshell falling into the batter.

Using a ball tin

For the sponge cakes used in this book, bake the cake in the ball tin in two halves. Allow the halves to cool in the tin and then level each cake using the edge of the tin as a guide. Stick the two halves together with buttercream to create a perfect sphere.

Madeira Cake Quantities

Cakes	Bakeware	Unsalted (sweet) butter	Caster (superfine) sugar	Self-raising (self-rising) flour	Plain (all-purpose) flour	Eggs (large) (US extra large)	Baking Times at 160°C/325°/ Gas 3
Spot On!	baked in a 1.5 litre (2½ pint) pudding bowl and 10cm (4in) round tin (pan)	350g (12oz)	350g (12oz)	350g (12oz)	175g (6oz)	6	1¼–1½ hours
Squeak with Delight	20cm (8in) round tin						
Tall Story							
Fleecy Fun	25.5cm (10in) round tin	500g (1lb 2oz)	500g (1lb 2oz)	500g (1lb 2oz)	250g (9oz)	9	1½–1¾ hours
Flower Power	25.5cm (10in) round tin						
Take It Easy **Bake two rectangular cakes**	25.5 x 20cm (10 x 8in) rectangular tin (multisized cake pan) plus 9cm (3½in) round tin	550g (1¼lb)	550g (1¼lb)	550g (1¼lb)	275g (10oz)	10	1½–1¾ hours
Top Dog	30 x 18cm (12 x 7in) rectangular tin						
Purrfectly Exotic	30 x 23cm (12 x 9in) rectangular tin (multisized cake pan)	700g (1½lb)	700g (1½lb)	700g (1½lb)	350g (12oz)	12	1¾–2 hours

Chocolate Cake Quantities

Cakes	Bakeware	Plain (semisweet) chocolate	Unsalted (sweet) butter	Caster (superfine) sugar	Eggs (large) (US extra large)	Icing (confectioners') sugar	Self-raising (self-rising) flour	Baking Times at 180°C/350°/ Gas 4
Vamp It Up!	13cm (5in) ball tin (pan)	175g (6oz)	115g (4oz)	75g (3oz)	4	25g (1oz)	115g (4oz)	45 mins–1 hour
Farmyard Feast	15 x 20cm (6 x 8in) rectangular tin (multisized cake pan)	275g (10oz)	225g (8oz)	150g (5oz)	8	50g (2oz)	225g (8oz)	1–1¼ hours
Whale of a Time	20 x 30cm (8 x 12in) rectangular tin	550g (1¼lb)	500g (1lb 2oz)	300g (11oz)	16	100g (3½oz)	500g (1lb 2oz)	1¾–2 hours
Cheeky Chimp	23cm (9in) round tin	425g (15oz)	275g (10oz)	175g (6oz)	10	70g (2½oz)	275g (10oz)	1¼–1½ hours
Roaring Success **Bake two**								
Prickly Visitor	25.5 x 20cm (10 x 8in) rectangular tin (multisized cake pan)	500g (1lb 2oz)	350g (12oz)	225g (8oz)	12	75g (3oz)	350g (12oz)	1½–1¾ hours
Pool Party	25.5cm (10in) round tin							

Cup Cakes

You can use any sponge cake recipe to bake cup cakes, but to avoid domed tops you will need to reduce the amount of flour used. As a general rule, reduce the flour by 15ml (1 tbsp) for every 150g (5oz) of flour in the recipe.

Vanilla cup cakes

The following recipe uses milk to soften the batter and produces a good, flat-topped cup cake.

Ingredients Makes 24

- ❀ 115g (4oz) butter
- ❀ 225g (8oz) caster (superfine) sugar
- ❀ 175g (6oz) plain (all-purpose) flour
- ❀ 7.5ml (1½ tsp) baking powder
- ❀ 2 eggs, at room temperature
- ❀ 125ml (4fl oz) milk
- ❀ 5ml (1 tsp) vanilla extract

Decorating the cup cakes

There are a number of ways of adding decorations to cup cakes but the method you choose will depend on the time you have available and the effect you are trying to create. In this book cup cakes are coordinated with some of the main cakes and have sugarpaste (rolled fondant) and modelling paste as the decoration mediums.

1 To cover the cup cakes with sugarpaste, roll out the sugarpaste to a thickness of 5mm (³/₁₆in) using spacers.

2 Select a circle cutter that has the same diameter as the top of the cup cakes and cut out the appropriate number of sugarpaste discs (**C**). Place the discs onto the cakes and then decorate as required.

1 Preheat the oven to 190°C/375°F/Gas 5. Place 24 paper baking cases in bun trays (muffin pans).

2 Cream the butter and sugar in a large mixing bowl until light, fluffy and pale. Sift the flour and baking powder into a separate bowl.

3 Beat the eggs into the creamed mixture, one at a time, following each with a spoonful of flour, to prevent the mixture curdling. Stir the remaining flour into the mixture, alternating with the milk. Stir in the vanilla extract.

4 Fill the paper cases half-full with the mixture (**A**). Bake for about 20 minutes, or until the tops of the cakes spring back when lightly touched. Leave to cool in the tray for 5 minutes, and then transfer to a cooling rack to cool completely (**B**).

These cute little curly fleeced sheep have been piped onto the sugarpaste topping using tinted buttercream.

Modelling paste paisley shapes defined with modelling paste lines make an unusual decoration for cup cakes.

Displaying cup cakes

If you decide to make a feature of your decorated cup cakes, why not display them in a stand designed for the purpose?

Mini-cakes

Delightful bitesize and mini-cakes are great fun to make and are ideal to give as presents. An ever-growing selection of bakeware is available that allows you to bake a number of small cakes at once.

Creating mini-cakes

1 Choose a recipe for your mini-cakes – either of the recipes on pages 8–9 work well – and preheat your oven. To prevent the cakes sticking to the tins (pans), grease the tins well then sprinkle on some flour, shake the flour to cover all the greased surfaces and remove the excess. (There are a number of products now on the market that are designed specifically to prevent cakes sticking in tins. Some are brushed on whereas others are sprayed.)

2 Make the cake batter following the recipe; the amount of mixture you will require will depend on the size and number of the cakes you are baking.

3 Half-fill each section of the cake tin with the mixture (**A**) and bake; the time required will depend on the size of the cakes, but as a guide mini-cakes usually take 15–20 minutes whereas bitesize cakes take 7–10 minutes. Leave the cakes to cool in the tin.

4 Level the cakes by taking a large knife and carving across the top of each cake, using the edge of the tin as a guide (**B**). Place the cakes on waxed paper with the shaped side uppermost, and cover with a thin layer of buttercream.

5 Roll some sugarpaste (rolled fondant) to a depth of 5mm (³/₁₆in). Lift the paste over the top of one cake. Smooth the surface of the cake to remove any lumps and bumps. Then take a smoother and, while pressing down, run the flat edge around the base of the cake to create a clean cutting line (**C**). Trim away the excess paste with a palette knife. Repeat for the remaining cakes.

Mini-cakes can dry out quickly so try not to leave them uncovered for any length of time.

6 Once the sugarpaste has dried, decorate as you like; for example, using thinly rolled modelling paste cut into shapes using cutters (**D**).

You can scale down the full-sized cake to make a perfect baby version complete with covered board.

Appealing and fun mini-cakes can be quite simple to make, such as these cheerful giraffes.

Cookies

Decorating cookies is a great way of getting children involved in party preparations. You will find that there is a huge assortment of cookie and biscuit cutters available so you should be able to pick some that will fit your theme.

Vanilla cookies

Ingredients Makes 22–24

- 275g (10oz) plain (all-purpose) flour, sifted
- 5ml (1 tsp) baking powder
- 100g (3½oz) caster (superfine) sugar
- 75g (3oz) butter, diced
- 1 small egg, beaten
- 30ml (2 tbsp) golden (light corn) syrup
- 2.5ml (½ tsp) vanilla extract

Decorating cookies

This can be done in a number of ways, depending on how much time you have available and what effect you wish to create.

Water icing and royal icing

These icings are used for similar effects, water icing, as used for the Dolphin Cookies, is a softer icing but royal icing, as used for the Dog Bone Cookies, produces stronger colours.

1 Divide your chosen icing into small bowls and tint with edible colours. Adjust the consistency, if necessary, so that the icing can be easily spread; add either a little icing (confectioners') sugar or water as required. Then cover with plastic wrap to prevent a skin forming.

2 Spread the icing over the cookies with a palette knife (**C**). Then, while the icing is still wet, either add your choice of ready-made decorations on top or place some contrasting icing into a piping bag and pipe a pattern into the wet icing (**D**). Leave until firm.

1 Preheat the oven to 160ºC/325ºF/Gas 3 and grease a baking sheet. Sift the dry ingredients into a large bowl.

2 Add the butter and rub together with your fingertips until the mixture resembles fine breadcrumbs.

3 Make a hollow in the centre and pour in the beaten egg, golden syrup and vanilla. Mix together well until you have a ball of dough. Place in a plastic bag and chill in the refrigerator for 30 minutes.

4 Roll out the dough on a lightly floured surface to 5mm (³/₁₆in) thick, and stamp out the cookies, using your chosen cutters (**A**). Lightly knead and re-roll the trimmings together, and cut out more cookies to use up all the dough. Place the cookies on the greased baking sheet.

5 Bake the cookies for 12–15 minutes, or until lightly coloured and firm but not crisp. Leave on the tray for 5 minutes before transferring to a wire rack to cool completely (**B**).

Make the cookies up to one month beforehand and store them un-iced in an airtight container in the freezer.

Modelling paste

Use thinly rolled modelling paste cut out with sugarcraft cutters to decorate shapes (**E**). Add coloured sweets and edible dragées (sugar balls) to add more interest, if you like.

Mould Making

The Take It Easy and Roaring Success cup cakes both use moulded animals as decorations. Commercial moulds tend to be expensive and often are not exactly what you require but it is quite easy to make your own.

Making and using a mould

You will need

✿ non-toxic modelling clay or Plasticine, available from toy and art stores
✿ Dresden tool and cutting wheel
✿ pot of moulding gel
✿ modelling paste
✿ edible paste colours
✿ clear spirit, such as gin or vodka
✿ paintbrushes

If making your own model sounds too much like hard work, try using fridge magnets, shells, buttons, jewellery, coins, children's toys, and so on.

1 To make the original model to be moulded, knead some modelling clay to warm it and build up the basic design using rolled shapes, and then blend and texture as appropriate. Make the model with a flat base. The picture (**A**) shows how the tiger's head has been built up from a half-ball shape by adding sausage and ball shapes, blended with a Dresden tool and textured with a cutting wheel.

2 Roll out some modelling clay, not too thinly, place the model in the centre, and then bring up the sides and pinch them together to form a container. Alternatively, make a container from aluminium foil or use a plastic beaker or small bowl.

3 Melt the moulding gel following the manufacturer's instructions on the pot, and then pour it into the container until the model is completely covered (**B**).

4 Leave until set (usually 5–10 minutes) and then carefully peel away the container. Turn the mould upside down and carefully remove the model from the base of the mould.

5 Knead some modelling paste to warm it and roll it into a ball. Press the ball firmly into the newly created mould, level the paste with the top of the mould and then carefully release (**C**). Repeat to make as many shapes as you need.

6 Once the moulded shapes are dry, dilute some paste colours in clear spirit and then paint as appropriate (**D**).

If your mould doesn't turn out quite as you had envisaged it, just re-melt it and try again. You can also reuse the gel after you have finished using it for a set of models.

Covering Boards and Cakes

Follow these basic techniques to achieve a neat and professional appearance to the initial cake and board coverings. With care and practice you will soon find that you have a perfectly smooth finish.

Levelling the cake

Making an accurate cake base is an important part of creating your masterpiece. There are two methods, depending on the cake you are using, so choose the easiest:

Method 1

Place a set square up against the edge of the cake and, with a knife, mark a line around the top of the cake at the required height, usually 7–7.5cm (2¾–3in) for the cakes in this book, but sometimes less. With a large serrated knife cut around the marked line and across the cake to remove the domed crust.

Method 2

Place a cake board into the base of the tin (pan) in which the cake was baked so that when the cake is placed on top the outer edge of the cake is level with the tin and the dome will protrude above. Take a long sharp knife and cut the dome from the cake, keeping the knife against the tin. This will ensure the cake is completely level (**A**).

Freezing cakes

Most, but not all, of the cake projects require the cakes to be frozen. This allows you not only to bake the cakes in advance but also to carve more intricate shapes without the cake crumbling and falling apart. How hard your cake freezes depends on the settings of your freezer, so it may be necessary to let your cake defrost slightly before attempting to carve it. Detailed carving instructions are given with each project.

Filling cakes

It is not necessary to add fillings to the cake recipes used in this book. However, many people do like their cakes filled with jam and/or buttercream. To add a filling split the cake into a number of horizontal layers and add your choice of filling. Tall Story illustrates one jam and one buttercream layer (**B**).

Covering cake boards

1 Knead the sugarpaste (rolled fondant) until warm and pliable. Roll out on a surface lightly dusted with icing (confectioners') sugar, or if you have a large corian work board or worktop use white vegetable fat (shortening) instead. White fat works well, and you don't have the problems of icing sugar drying out or marking the sugarpaste. Roll out the sugarpaste to a depth of 4mm (⅛in), ideally using spacers (**C**).

2 Moisten the board with water or sugar glue. Using a rolling pin, lift up the paste and drape over the board (**D**). Circle a smoother over the paste to achieve a smooth, flat finish to the board. Cut the paste flush with the sides of the board using a palette knife, taking care to keep the edge vertical (**E**). Leave the covered board overnight to dry thoroughly.

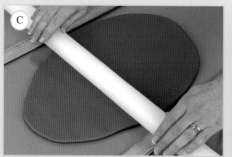

Applying a sugarpaste covering

1 Place the cake either on a sheet of waxed paper or directly onto a covered dried sugarpaste (rolled fondant) board. Prepare the cake by covering it with a thin layer of buttercream to fill in any holes and help the sugarpaste stick. Brush away the excess crumbs. (Waxed paper cut to the same shape as the cake and placed between the surface of the board and the cake will prevent the icing under the cake getting sticky.)

2 Knead the sugarpaste until warm and pliable. Roll the paste to a depth of 5mm (³⁄₁₆in). It is a good idea to use spacers for this, as they ensure an even thickness.

3 Lift the paste carefully over the top of the cake, supporting it with a rolling pin, and position it so that it covers the cake (**F**).

4 Smooth the surface of the cake to remove any lumps and bumps using a smoother for the flat areas and a combination of smoother and the palm of your hand for the curved ones. Always make sure your hands are clean and dry with no traces of icing (confectioners') sugar before smoothing sugarpaste. Take the smoother and, while pressing down, run the flat edge around the base of the cake to create a cutting line (**G**). Trim away the excess paste with a palette knife (**H**).

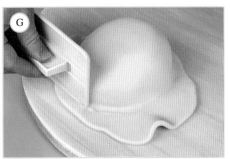

If you find you have unwanted air bubbles under the icing, insert a clean glass-headed dressmakers' pin at an angle and press out the air.

You can make your own spacers from strip wood available from DIY stores.

Cake crumb idea – Chocolate Truffle Cheesecake

When making novelty cakes you are always left with cake crumbs. They can be used in a deliciously rich Chocolate Truffle Cheesecake. Break 175g (6oz) plain (semisweet) chocolate into a heatproof bowl over a pan of hot water. Stir until the chocolate has melted. Soften 225g (8oz) full-fat soft cheese in a large bowl. Beat in 100g (3½oz) caster (superfine) sugar and 60ml (4 tbsp) rum until the mixture is light and creamy. Stir in the melted chocolate, 100g (3½oz) cake crumbs, 75g (3oz) chopped walnuts and 100g (3½oz) chopped glacé (candied) cherries. If the mixture is too soft to handle, chill, then mould it into a small log shape. Coat the shape evenly with 75g (3oz) chocolate curls. Chill for one hour. Decorate with extra glacé cherries and walnuts, if you like.

Sugar Recipes

Most of the sugar recipes used in the book for covering, modelling and decoration can easily be made at home. Use paste colours to colour them according to the individual project.

Sugarpaste

Ready-made sugarpaste (rolled fondant) can be obtained from supermarkets and cake-decorating suppliers, and is available in white and the whole colour spectrum. It is also easy and inexpensive to make your own.

Ingredients Makes 1kg (2¼lb)
✿ 60ml (4 tbsp) cold water
✿ 20ml (4 tsp/1 sachet) powdered gelatine
✿ 125ml (4fl oz) liquid glucose
✿ 15ml (1 tbsp) glycerine
✿ 1kg (2¼lb) icing (confectioners') sugar, sieved, plus extra for dusting

1 Place the water in a small bowl, sprinkle over the gelatine and soak until spongy. Stand the bowl over a pan of hot, but not boiling, water and stir until the gelatine is dissolved. Add the glucose and glycerine, stirring until well blended and runny.

2 Put the icing sugar in a large bowl, make a well in the centre and slowly pour in the liquid ingredients, stirring constantly. Mix well. Turn out onto a surface dusted with icing sugar and knead until smooth, sprinkling with extra icing sugar if the paste becomes too sticky. The paste can be used immediately or tightly wrapped and stored in a plastic bag.

You can buy vegetarian gelatine from supermarkets.

Modelling paste

This versatile paste keeps its shape well, dries harder than sugar-paste (rolled fondant) and is used throughout the book for adding detail to covered cakes. There are commercial varieties available, but is easy and a lot cheaper to make your own paste.

Ingredients Makes 225g (8oz)
✿ 5ml (1 tsp) gum tragacanth
✿ 225g (8oz) sugarpaste (rolled fondant)

Add the gum tragacanth to the sugarpaste and knead in. Wrap in a plastic bag and allow the gum to work before use. You will begin to feel a difference in the paste after an hour or so, but it is best left overnight. The modelling paste should be firm but pliable with a slight elastic texture. Kneading the modelling paste makes it warm and easy to work with.

Modelling-paste tips
✿ Gum tragacanth is a natural gum available from cake-decorating suppliers used for hardening icing.
✿ If time is short use CMC instead of gum tragacanth. This is a synthetic product but it works almost immediately.
✿ Placing your modelling paste in a microwave for a few seconds is an excellent way of warming it for use.
✿ If you have previously added a large amount of colour to your paste and it is consequently too soft, an extra pinch or two of gum tragacanth will be necessary.
✿ If your paste is dry, crumbly or too hard to work, add a touch of white vegetable fat (shortening) and a little boiled water, and knead until softened.
✿ Use the paste while fresh or immediately if made with CMC.

Pastillage

This is an extremely useful paste because, unlike modelling paste, it sets extremely hard and is not affected by moisture the way other pastes are. However, the paste crusts quickly and is brittle once dry. You can buy it in a powdered form, to which you add water, but it is easy to make yourself.

Ingredients Makes 350g (12oz)
✿ 1 egg white
✿ 300g (11oz) icing (confectioners') sugar, sifted
✿ 10ml (2 tsp) gum tragacanth

1 Put the egg white into a large mixing bowl. Gradually add enough icing sugar until the mixture combines together into a ball. Mix in the gum tragacanth, and then turn the paste out onto a work surface and knead the pastillage well.

2 Incorporate the remaining icing sugar into the remainder of pastillage to give a stiff paste.

3 Store pastillage in a polythene bag placed in an airtight container in a refrigerator for up to one month.

Colouring paste
To colour paste, place a little paste colour, not liquid colour, onto the end of a cocktail stick (toothpick) or a larger amount onto the end of a palette knife. Add to the paste and knead in thoroughly, adding more until you have the correct result. Be careful with pale colours, as only a little colour is needed.

Sugar sense – back to basics

Sugarpaste (rolled fondant) Used for covering boards and cakes

Modelling paste Used to add decoration to cakes or to create models

Pastillage Used for all the bits that stick out of a cake, such as antennae and whiskers, and for creating firm, edible supports

Buttercream Used to fill and coat cakes and sometimes used as a covering

Buttercream

Use buttercream to sandwich cakes together, to coat them before covering with sugarpaste (rolled fondant) or on its own as a cake covering.

Ingredients Makes 1 quantity

✿ 110g (3¾oz) unsalted (sweet) butter
✿ 350g (12oz) icing (confectioners') sugar
✿ 15–30ml (1–2 tbsp) milk or water
✿ a few drops of vanilla extract or alternative flavouring

1 Place the butter in a bowl and beat until the texture is light and fluffy.

2 Sift the icing sugar into the bowl and continue to beat until the mixture changes colour. Add just enough milk or water to give a firm but spreadable consistency.

3 Flavour by adding the vanilla or alternative flavouring, then store in an airtight container until required.

White buttercream

This is a useful alternative for those on a dairy-free diet. Simply follow the buttercream recipe but replace the butter with solid white vegetable fat (shortening).

Chocolate buttercream

To make chocolate buttercream, follow the buttercream recipe above and mix 30ml (2 tbsp) of unsweetened cocoa powder with the milk or water before adding it to the butter and sugar mixture. Omit the flavourings.

White chocolate buttercream

Ingredients Makes 1 quantity

✿ 115g (4oz) white chocolate
✿ 115g (4oz) unsalted (sweet) butter
✿ 225g (8oz) icing (confectioners') sugar

Melt the chocolate in a bowl over a pan of hot water and leave to cool slightly. Soften the butter and beat in the sugar, and then beat in the chocolate.

Royal icing

Ingredients Makes 1 quantity

✿ 1 egg white
✿ 250g (9oz) icing (confectioners') sugar, sifted

Put the egg white into a bowl and gradually beat in the icing sugar until the icing is glossy and forms soft peaks.

Water icing

Ingredients Makes 1 quantity

✿ 450g (1lb) icing (confectioners') sugar

This is useful for icing cookies. Make water icing by putting 20–90ml (4tsp–6 tbsp) very hot water from the kettle into a bowl. Sift over the icing sugar and mix to a spreadable consistency, adding more water if necessary.

Piping gel

This is used when a wet liquid effect is required; for example, animals' eyes as for Roaring Success, water droplets as for Pool Party and Top Dog, or for water as on the waves of Whale of a Time. Piping gel is available from cake-decorating suppliers.

White vegetable fat (shortening)

This is a solid white vegetable fat, which is often known by a brand name: in the UK, Trex or White Flora; in South Africa, Holsum; in Australia, Copha; and in America, Crisco. These products are more or less interchangeable in cake making.

Confectioners' glaze

Used where a glossy-looking sheen is needed; for example, on eyes such as on Take It Easy, and where a surface needs sealing such as for the waves of Whale of a Time. Confectioners' glaze is available from cake-decorating suppliers.

Sugar glue

Although commercially available, sugar glue is quick and easy to make at home.

Break up pieces of white modelling paste into an eggcup or small bowl and cover with boiling water. Stir until dissolved. This produces a thick, strong glue, which can be easily thinned by adding some more cooled boiled water. If strong glue is required, use pastillage rather than modelling paste as the base (useful for delicate work, but not needed for any projects in this book).

Sugar Crystal Growing

Growing sugar crystals is great fun and an ideal activity for children to be involved in. As crystals take several weeks or even months to grow, you need to be patient.

You will need
✿ 500ml/18fl oz water (distilled works best but is not essential)
✿ pan
✿ 600–750g (1lb 5oz–1lb 10oz) granulated sugar
✿ 1 tall empty glass jar
✿ string
✿ paper clip
✿ 1 barbecue skewer or dowel

1 Boil the water in the pan then turn off the heat.

2 Gradually add the sugar to the hot water, a spoonful at a time, and stir after each addition to dissolve the sugar. Continue gradually adding the sugar until no more will dissolve. If necessary reheat the solution to make it clear.

3 Cool the sugar solution slightly and then pour it into the tall glass jar. Leave to reach room temperature.

4 Cut a length of string to the height of the jar. Attach a weight such as a paper clip to one end and tie the other around the skewer or dowel. Moisten the string with water and seed the string by rubbing grains of sugar along its length. Allow the string to dry.

5 Carefully lower the string into the jar so that the weight rests above the base, and then rest the skewer across the rim (**A**).

6 Leave undisturbed for several weeks or months. You should see crystals growing within 2–5 days, although it might take a little longer. The picture shows crystals after 2 weeks (**B**).

7 You will find that after a while the crystals will stop growing, so if you want to create large specimens, remove the string of crystals from the jar and separate the crystals from the string; they should separate quite easily. Cut and moisten a new string then select a number of crystals, place these on the string and allow the string to dry.

8 Pour the sugar solution back into the pan and heat as before then add more sugar as before until the solution is saturated. Allow to cool, then lower the string with the specimen crystals into the jar (**C**) and allow to grow (**D**).

You could colour the sugar solution with edible liquid colours and create tinted or coloured crystals, depending on how much colour you add.

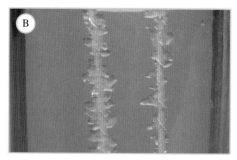

Using your crystals
Home-grown crystals are used in this book to represent diamanté for the collar in Purrfectly Exotic (right) by painting the back of the crystals with edible silver lustre dust (far right), but the possibilities for their use are endless. They make unusual sparkly centres for flowers, they can also be used for rocks beneath a fantasy castle or would look fun on a Christmas cake to create an icy scene.

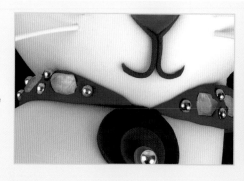

Decorations and Storage

You can experiment with a variety of decorations available to the sugarcrafter to enhance your cakes. Store your final creation carefully to ensure that it remains in perfect condition before it is served.

Edible decorations

There is an ever-increasing variety of ready-made decorations available from supermarkets and sugarcraft suppliers, and, used wisely, they are a great way of saving time and adding that extra touch. Dragées (sugar balls) add a touch of glamour and opulence to the cakes, as can be seen in Purrfectly Exotic.

Candles

No child's birthday cake would be complete without candles. There is a huge assortment of styles available covering the complete colour spectrum as well as fun novelty candles. Choose your candles carefully to complement the cake, and remember that the candles do not have to be placed on the cake itself, they can be positioned on the board using commercial holders or set into modelling-paste balls or shapes, such as flowers, hearts or stars.

Glittery stars make great candleholders for Vamp It Up!

Storage

Protect your cake by placing it in a clean, covered cake box and store somewhere cool and dry, but never in a refrigerator. If the box is slightly larger than the cake and the cake is to be transported, use non-slip matting to prevent the cake moving.

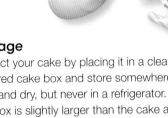

The following conditions will affect your decorated cake:

✿ Sunlight will fade and alter the colours of icing, so always store in a dark place.
✿ Humidity can have a disastrous effect on decorations, causing the icing to become soft and models to droop.
✿ Heat can melt icing, especially buttercream.

The Cakes

Prickly Visitor

He might be covered in prickles but this gorgeous hedgehog would be the most welcome guest at a party. Chocolate cake is simply carved to shape and then partially covered with sugarpaste for this straightforward cake. The delicious prickles are made from flaked chocolate, giving the hedgehog a perfect appearance. Apart from making a great cake for a child's birthday, the hedgehog would be a fun choice for a gardener's birthday or for anyone who is enthusiastic about wildlife. A spiky mini-cake accompanies the main cake.

Materials

- ✿ 25.5 × 20cm (10 × 8in) rectangular chocolate cake (see pages 8–9) (use a multisized tin)
- ✿ 2 × quantities chocolate buttercream
- ✿ paste colours: golden brown (Spectral – Autumn Leaf), dark brown
- ✿ sugarpaste (rolled fondant): 800g (1¾lb) ivory or white, 200g (7oz) brown
- ✿ icing (confectioners') sugar (optional)
- ✿ white vegetable fat (shortening)
- ✿ gum tragacanth
- ✿ 48 flaked chocolate bars
- ✿ modelling paste: 15g (½oz) white, 25g (1oz) black
- ✿ sugar glue

Equipment

- ✿ greaseproof paper
- ✿ glass-headed dressmakers' pins
- ✿ 5mm (³⁄₁₆in) spacers
- ✿ 30cm (12in) round cake drum (board)
- ✿ smoother
- ✿ palette knife
- ✿ cocktail sticks (toothpicks)
- ✿ waxed paper
- ✿ small pair of scissors
- ✿ small pieces of foam
- ✿ craft knife
- ✿ oval cutters: 4.5cm (1¾in) (FMM geometric set), 2.8cm (1³⁄₃₂in), 2.3cm (¹⁵⁄₁₆in)
- ✿ cutting wheel
- ✿ narrow spacers made from 1.5mm (¹⁄₁₆in) thick card
- ✿ golden-brown ribbon and non-toxic glue stick

Preparation

Preparing the head cake for freezing

1 Level the cake to a height of 6.5cm (2½in), then cut it in half to give two 13 × 20cm (5 × 8in) rectangles. Spread buttercream over the top of one cake and stack the second on top. Make outline and profile templates from greaseproof paper and place the outline template on top of the stacked cake. With a large knife, cut vertically around the template (**A**).

2 Using dressmakers' pins to secure, place the profile template onto one side of the cake. Holding the knife horizontally, cut away the cake along the outline of the template (**B**). Freeze the cake overnight.

Covering the board

1 Using the golden-brown paste colour, colour the ivory or white sugarpaste five shades of golden brown. Break the coloured paste into small pieces and scatter them over your work surface to mix up the colours. Gather the scattered pieces together into a ball and briefly knead together. Cut across the ball to reveal the marbled pattern inside.

2 Place the two halves next to one another and then roll the paste out between the 5mm (³⁄₁₆in) spacers using icing sugar or white vegetable fat to prevent sticking (**C**). The direction in which you roll the paste will affect the resulting marbled pattern, so try altering the direction you are rolling as the pattern develops. Lift up the paste, using a rolling pin for support, and place it over the cake board. Take a smoother and, using a circular motion, smooth the paste to give a level surface. Using a palette knife, trim the edges flush with the sides of the board, taking care to keep the cut vertical. Place to one side to dry.

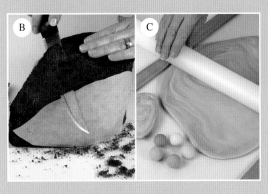

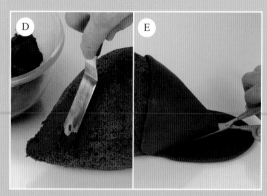

Making modelling paste

Take 50g (2oz) of golden-brown sugarpaste trimmings and knead in 1.5ml (¼ tsp) gum tragacanth to make modelling paste. Leave the modelling paste to mature, ideally overnight.

Stage One

Carving the cake

1 Remove the cake from the freezer. Insert cocktail sticks in a central line over the top of the cake. To create the curved appearance to the cake, cut from the central line of cocktail sticks to the horizontal buttercream line around the sides, where the two sections of cake meet, using a curved cut.

2 Then curve all the cut edges of the snout to shape (see picture D). Finally, remove a wedge of cake from below the horizontal line all the way around the base.

Cut away small pieces of cake at a time to avoid removing too much.

Covering the cake

1 Colour the buttercream a darker shade of brown using the dark brown food colour. Place the cake on waxed paper and spread a thin layer of buttercream over the face area (D).

2 Knead the brown sugarpaste until warm then roll out between the 5mm (³⁄₁₆in) spacers and place over the buttercreamed area of cake. Ease in the fullness of paste around the sides of the cake and bring the excess together under the snout. Cut away this excess paste using a small pair of scissors (E). Smooth the paste firstly with a smoother and then use the heat of your hand to create an even surface. Cut away the excess paste at the base with a palette knife and then remove the excess from around the face (F).

Adding the spines

1 Cover the front half of the body of the hedgehog with a thick layer of buttercream (G). Take a chopping board and sharp knife, and unwrap the bars of flaked chocolate. Place the chocolate on the chopping board and cut in half, then split each half lengthways into three or four sections (H).

2 Insert a row of spines into the cake centrally from one side of the hedgehog to the other by pushing the spines gently into the cake until they are held securely (I). Next, insert a row of spines from the spine in the centre of the back to the face, decreasing the size and changing the angle as the spines come down towards the face. Now fill the marker spines with spines of the appropriate size, referring to the picture for guidance (J).

You may find it easier to chill the chocolate in the refrigerator before splitting.

3 Carefully transfer the cake to the covered cake board. Cover the remaining cake with a thick layer of buttercream and insert the flaked chocolate as before. To prevent the spines from falling at the back before the buttercream sets, support them as necessary with small pieces of foam (K). Leave to set.

Stage Two

Decorating the cake

Eyes Individually roll out some of the white, golden-brown and black modelling paste. Cut two 4.5cm (1¾in) ovals from the white modelling paste, two 3cm (1¹⁄₈in) from the golden-brown modelling paste and two 2.3cm (¹⁵⁄₁₆in) from the black modelling paste. Place the golden-brown and black ovals at one end of the larger white ovals, as shown (**L**), and cut away the excess with the largest oval cutter. Shape the lower edge of the white of the eye with a cutting wheel, remembering that the eyes should be mirror images of each other. Cut a small white triangle and add to the top of each eye for a light spot. Attach in place on the cake using sugar glue to secure.

Whiskers and eyelashes Roll out the black modelling paste between the narrow spacers, then take the cutting wheel and run it backwards and forwards through the paste to create long, thin triangles (**M**). Cut across the base of the triangles and arrange three on either side of the snout, secure in place with sugar glue and support each with a glass-headed dressmakers' pin until dry (**N**). For the lashes attach two smaller triangles to the corner of each eye and turn the ends up slightly to curve.

Nose Knead a small amount of golden-brown sugarpaste until warm, adding a little white vegetable fat and boiled water to soften if necessary. Then roll the paste into a ball and attach to the tip of the cake (see picture N).

If you are experiencing problems attaching the nose, insert a small length of uncooked spaghetti into the tip of the cake and place the ball on top. The spaghetti will help to anchor the ball.

Finishing touches
Using a non-toxic glue stick, attach the golden-brown ribbon around the sides of the board to complete the cake.

Animal Magic

Personalize the cake by using letter cutters to add a name, age and/or 'Happy Birthday' to the board.

❁

Change the shape of the cake slightly to create a porcupine.

❁

Don't feel restricted to using flaked chocolate – use whatever takes your fancy: chocolate finger biscuits (cookies), chocolate buttons, chocolate sticks or, for an especially wacky hedgehog, use multicoloured candy sticks.

❁

Mini-cakes
Cover the required number of 18cm (7in) cake boards with marbled sugarpaste and leave to dry. Bake half-ball-shaped mini-cakes using the mini-ball or Mini-wonder Mold cake pans (W) following the instructions on page 11. Working on one cake at a time, place a cake onto a covered cake board and cover with dark brown chocolate buttercream. Roll 75g (3oz) of brown sugarpaste into a ball and then a cone. Slightly hollow out the wider end with your thumb and stick to your mini-cake for a head. Take 300g (11oz) of mint- or orange-flavoured chocolate sticks and break them into pieces, the largest approximately 4cm (1½in) long. Insert the sticks into the cake as for the main cake and leave to dry in place. Add a face, as for the main cake, but use smaller cutters. Repeat to make a family of hedgehogs, if you like.

Spot On!

No one could resist inviting this far-from-ugly bug to the ball, with its adorable little smile, funky antennae, giant dots and bright red wings. This cute ladybird, or ladybug, cake will have instant appeal and is perfect for a small child's birthday, but might also be suitable for an adult who loves gardening – or just ladybirds. The project is quite simple and even the leaf the insect sits on is easily achieved by using a cabbage leaf to print its impression into sugarpaste. Make brightly coloured butterfly, flower or ladybird cookies to accompany the cake.

Materials

- ❀ Madeira cake made with 6 eggs and baked in a 1.5 litre (2½ pint) pudding bowl and 10cm (4in) round tin (see pages 8–9)
- ❀ modelling paste: 125g (4½oz) black, 25g (1oz) white
- ❀ sugarpaste (rolled fondant): 800g (1¾lb) green, 100g (3½oz) white, 250g (9oz) black, 500g (1lb 2oz) red
- ❀ icing (confectioners') sugar (optional)
- ❀ sugar glue
- ❀ white vegetable fat (shortening)
- ❀ paste colours: green, black
- ❀ clear spirit – gin or vodka
- ❀ small amount of pastillage
- ❀ 1 quantity buttercream

Equipment

- ❀ greaseproof paper
- ❀ glass-headed pins
- ❀ 30 × 25.5cm (12in × 10in) oval cake drum (board)
- ❀ palette knife
- ❀ craft knife
- ❀ cabbage leaf, such as Savoy
- ❀ flat-headed and fine paintbrushes
- ❀ sugar shaper with large and small round discs
- ❀ cocktail stick (toothpick)
- ❀ waxed paper
- ❀ smoother
- ❀ 5mm (³/₁₆in) spacers
- ❀ cutting wheel
- ❀ sharp scissors
- ❀ Dresden tool
- ❀ narrow spacers made from 1.5mm (¹/₁₆in) thick card
- ❀ circle cutters: 4.5cm (1¾in), 3.5cm (1⅜in)
- ❀ oval cutters: 1.9cm (¾in), 1.6cm (⅝in)
- ❀ no. 16 piping tube (tip)
- ❀ dowel
- ❀ black ribbon and non-toxic glue stick

Preparation

Preparing the head cake for freezing

1 Make two head templates using greaseproof paper. Place the templates either side of the 10cm (4in) round head cake, securing in place with pins. With one template facing you, hold a knife with the blade reaching from one template to the other and cut the cake along the edges of the template (**A**).

2 Remove the templates and reposition them onto the cake that has just been shaped, and cut as before. You should now have a rough square-shaped dome. Freeze the cake until firm, ideally overnight.

Covering the board

1 Draw the outline of the central section of a large leaf onto the cake drum using a pencil. Thinly roll out some of the black modelling paste, cut it into strips, and, using sugar glue or water, stick the strips to the board around the outer edges of the drawn leaf. Trim the edges flush with the sides of the board, using a palette knife.

2 Knead the green sugarpaste, and then roll it out, using icing sugar or white fat to prevent it sticking. Paint sugar glue or water over the uncovered surface of the board, and cover the whole board with the rolled out sugarpaste. Remove the sugarpaste from the top of the black areas with a knife.

3 Take a dry cabbage leaf and press the veins on the underside of the leaf gently into the soft paste. Repeat, positioning the veins to create one large leaf (**B**). Using a palette knife, trim the edges of the leaf flush with the sides of the board. Place to one side to dry. Dilute some green paste colour in clear spirit and, with a flat-headed paintbrush, paint over the leaf to highlight the texture (**C**).

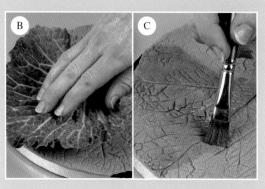

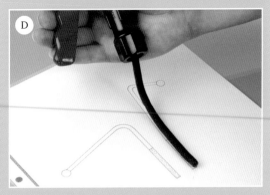

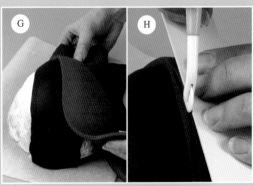

Antennae

Trace the antennae templates onto plain paper. Colour the pastillage black, then knead in some white fat and place in a sugar shaper with the large round disc. The pastillage should be soft to work in the sugar shaper, add a little boiled water to soften if necessary. Squeeze the pastillage onto the templates and cut to size (**D**). Allow to dry thoroughly – an airing cupboard is an ideal place to dry pastillage.

Stage One

Carving the cake

1 Remove the head cake from the freezer. Mark the top with a cocktail stick. Take a small knife and remove the corners by carving down from the cocktail stick to the lower edge to create a symmetrical shape.

2 Take the body cake and level to just above where it has risen in the bowl. Place the cake on the levelled surface and remove the crust from the side of the cake. Adjust the shape as necessary to make a rounded dome shape, leaving the top flat (**E**). Remove a 1.5cm (⁹⁄₁₆in) wedge of cake from around the base of the cake. Remove a section of cake from the head to allow the two cakes to abut.

Covering the cake

1 Place the body cake on waxed paper and spread over a thin layer of buttercream to stick the sugarpaste, then create a rounded appearance to the top of the cake by adding some white sugarpaste. Shape the paste and blend the edges into the cake using a smoother and then the palm of your hand (see picture F).

2 Roll out the black sugarpaste between the 5mm (³⁄₁₆in) spacers and cut into an 8cm (3¹⁄₈in) wide strip. Place the strip over the top of the body and blend the edges into the cake with a smoother (**F**). Cut away the excess paste at the base.

3 Roll out the red sugarpaste between the 5mm (³⁄₁₆in) spacers into a rough circle and cut in half. Place one half over one side of the body so that it rests centrally on the black strip on one side and near the outer edge of the black strip on the other side (**G**). Using a straightedge and a cutting wheel, cut the edge of the wing straight across the back (**H**). Soften the cut edge by running a finger along its length. Ease the paste at the base of the cake under the lip of the shell and cut away the excess with a palette knife. Repeat for the second wing then leave to dry.

4 Place the head cake on waxed paper and spread a thin layer of buttercream over to stick the sugarpaste. Roll out the black sugarpaste between the 5mm (³⁄₁₆in) spacers and cover the head. Gather the paste at the back of the head and cut away the excess with scissors; there is no need to neaten it. Cut off the excess paste at the base of the head and place to one side to dry.

Stage Two

Decorating the cake

Place the covered cakes onto the board at an angle to the stem of the leaf, with the head resting on the leaf. If necessary take some black sugarpaste and fill any gaps between the head and body. Smooth the paste at the back of the head with the smooth side of a Dresden tool to blend it into the paste of the head and body.

White patches Roll out the white modelling paste between the narrow spacers and cut two 4.5cm (1¾in) circles. Make a straight cut 1cm (³⁄₈in) in from one side of each circle (**I**) and place either side of the face so that the straight edge abuts the leaf. Smooth the cut edge with a finger.

Eyes Roll out the black and white modelling pastes between the narrow spacers then cut out two white 2cm (¾in) ovals, two black 1.6cm (⅝in) ovals and two white light spots using the no.16 piping tube. Attach the shapes to the front of the face.

Mouth Soften some white modelling paste by kneading in some white vegetable fat to stop the paste becoming sticky, then partially dunk the paste into a small container of boiled water before kneading again to achieve the consistency of chewing gum. Place the paste with the small round disc into the sugar shaper and squeeze out a length. With sugar glue and a fine paintbrush paint a smile onto the mouth area of the cake. Place the length of paste over the glue mouth and trim to size. Paint on the corners of the mouth and add small lengths of paste, and trim.

Legs Soften some black modelling paste as before, and place into the sugar shaper with the large round disc. Squeeze out two lengths and attach one end of each to the back of the head and the other to the front of the face. Arrange the legs into an 'L' shape (see main picture). Roll two 1.5cm (⁹⁄₁₆in) balls from black modelling paste, elongate and flatten each slightly, and place on top of the legs on the side of the face.

Spots Roll out the black modelling paste between the narrow spacers then cut out eight 3.5cm (1³⁄₈in) circles (**J**). Attach to the shell in a symmetrical arrangement.

Antennae Roll two 1.3cm (½in) balls from black sugarpaste. Insert a dowel into the centre of each to create a hole. Place some sugar glue on the end of the antennae and place the balls on top. Take a Dresden tool and blend the sugarpaste of the ball into the pastillage so that there is no join. Decide on the placement of the antennae and insert a dowel into the cake in these positions. Remove the dowel and position the antennae into the holes created in the cake.

Finishing touches
To give the shell and head a shiny appearance, spread over a very thin layer of white fat using a flat-headed paintbrush. Using a non-toxic glue stick, attach the ribbon around the sides of the board to complete the cake.

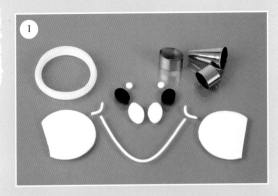

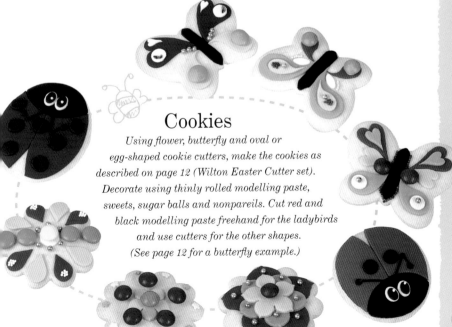

Cookies

Using flower, butterfly and oval or egg-shaped cookie cutters, make the cookies as described on page 12 (Wilton Easter Cutter set). Decorate using thinly rolled modelling paste, sweets, sugar balls and nonpareils. Cut red and black modelling paste freehand for the ladybirds and use cutters for the other shapes. (See page 12 for a butterfly example.)

Animal Magic

Personalize the cake by using letter cutters and modelling paste to add a name, age and/or 'Happy Birthday' to the board.

Use black sugarpaste to make the insect into a beetle, and add green or purple edible lustre dusts to the shell to give it an iridescent finish. Alternatively, look at pictures of brightly striped beetles and copy their markings.

Fleecy Fun

Invite this adorable sheep, with her soft fleece of golden curls, to celebrate a birthday or springtime party. This is a cake for buttercream fans, as it is covered entirely with layers of buttercream whirls. Although the cake is carved, it is a simple shape to achieve and, once you have mastered the buttercream curls, is straightforward and quite quick to make. It is sure to appeal to any small child – farm animals are always a favourite – and adults, too, will be captivated by its charm. The cute little cup cakes continue the theme.

Materials

✿ 25.5cm (10in) Madeira cake (see pages 8–9)

✿ sugarpaste (rolled fondant): 900g (2lb) purple-blue

✿ icing (confectioners') sugar or white vegetable fat (shortening)

✿ 3 quantities buttercream

✿ paste colours: golden brown (Spectral – Autumn Leaf), cream, dark brown

Equipment

✿ greaseproof paper

✿ glass-headed dressmakers' pins

✿ cocktail sticks (toothpicks)

✿ 5mm ($^3/_{16}$in) spacers

✿ 30cm (12in) square cake drum (board)

✿ smoother

✿ palette knife

✿ paintbrushes including a soft flat-headed brush

✿ reusable piping bag and coupler

✿ piping tubes (tips): nos 17, 4, 2

✿ scriber (optional)

✿ straightedge

✿ blue ribbon and non-toxic glue stick

Preparation

Preparing the head cake for freezing

Level the cake. Make a template from greaseproof paper and place on top of the cake and secure with pins. With a knife, cut vertically through the cake around the edge of the template (**A**). Insert cocktail sticks along the line around the head (**B**), then carefully lift off the template. Take a large knife and reduce the height of the body by 2cm (¾in) by cutting horizontally up to the cocktail sticks, so that the face stands proud (**C**). Remove the cocktail sticks and freeze the cake overnight.

Covering the board

Knead the purple-blue sugarpaste until warm. Then roll out between the 5mm ($^3/_{16}$in) spacers using icing sugar or white vegetable fat to prevent sticking. Lift up the paste, using a rolling pin for support, and place it over the board. Take a smoother and, using a circular motion, smooth the paste to give a level surface. Using a palette knife, trim the edges flush with the sides of the board, taking care to keep the cut vertical. Place to one side to dry.

Stage One

Carving the cake

Remove the cake from the freezer. To create a curved appearance to the cake, cut from the top central area down to the base of the cake using curved cuts. Then curve all the cut edges of the head to complete the cake (see picture E).

Covering the cake

Apply a crumb-coat of buttercream to the cake using a palette knife, and then transfer the cake to the covered board.

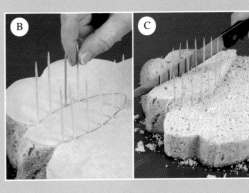

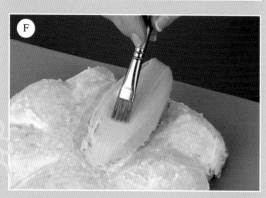

The head

1 Colour a half-quantity of buttercream a rich shade of golden brown using the golden-brown food colour. Add a little boiled water if necessary, to give the mixture a thick but easily spreadable consistency. Paddle the buttercream with a palette knife to exclude as many air bubbles as possible (**D**). Place some of the buttercream onto the head and spread with a palette knife into a thick and even layer (**E**).

2 To smooth the buttercream, have a pan of simmering water nearby and a soft flat-headed paintbrush. Start by taking the brush and dipping it into the hot water to heat it, this prevents the icing sticking to the brush, then remove the excess water. Smooth the icing by making long, smooth strokes down the face with the heated brush (**F**). Continue heating the brush and smoothing the icing until all the icing has been smoothed.

The body

1 Colour half the remaining buttercream using the cream paste colours, so that you have three colours: a little golden brown, cream and uncoloured.

2 Fit a coupler to a reusable piping bag and attach a no. 17 tube. Half-fill the bag with the three colours of buttercream, using mainly the cream and uncoloured and only a small amount of golden brown.

3 Using even pressure on the bag, start to pipe circular swirls onto the body of the cake (**G**). Start at the centre of the swirl and wrap the icing around onto itself as it emerges. Finish the swirl once it is three piped-lines deep, and neaten the end if necessary with a hot brush. Repeat until the whole of the body is covered in swirls, placing the swirls so that they neatly interlock.

4 Change the piping tube in the coupler to a no. 4 and pressure-pipe uncoloured buttercream in-between each of the swirls to fill the gaps and raise the level of the gaps ready for the second layer (see picture H). Allow the buttercream time to set.

Stage Two

Second layer of wool

Pipe a second layer of swirls over the gaps between the first layer of swirls (**H**). Leave space between these swirls so that the first layer is still visible. Leave to dry.

Eyes

1 Using a no. 17 tube and uncoloured buttercream, pipe two large dots for eyes and smooth the top with a hot brush (see picture J).

2 Colour a small amount of buttercream dark brown. Using a clean piping bag and a no. 4 tube, pipe pupils onto the lower half of each eye.

Nose

Using the no. 4 tube and the dark brown buttercream, pipe a 2cm (¾in) wide heart shape at the lower edge of the face to represent the nose. Smooth to shape with a hot brush. Change the tube to a no. 2 and pipe a vertical line down from the tip of the nose.

Legs

Darken the remaining golden-brown buttercream, and place into the piping bag and attach the no.17 piping tube. Using a scriber or pin and a straightedge, mark two straight lines onto the board, to act as a piping guide for the legs. Place the piping tube a fraction away from the body and squeeze the bag until the buttercream squeezed out is twice the diameter of the tube. Move the tube a fraction away from the body and squeeze again. Move and squeeze repeatedly to get a wrinkled/textured effect (**I**). Continue until the edge of the board is reached. Repeat for the second leg.

Ears

1 Make ear templates from greaseproof paper and attach them to the top of the head using glass-headed dressmakers' pins. Prick around the outline of each ear using a scriber or pin (**J**) and then remove the templates.

2 Using the darkened buttercream, pipe two buttercream lines along the ear inside the outline plus one line on top of the first two (**K**). Then, using a heated soft flat-headed brush, smooth the buttercream to shape (**L**). Repeat for the second ear.

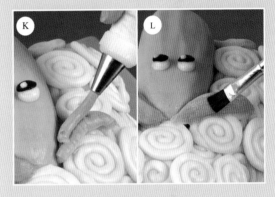

Finishing touches

Add a dot of uncoloured buttercream to the pupil of each eye to act as a light spot (see main picture). Using a non-toxic glue stick attach the ribbon around the sides of the board to complete the cake.

Animal Magic

If you are not partial to buttercream, create the cake using sugarpaste, and form the swirls using a sugar shaper fitted with the large round disc.

Add horns to create a ram.

To save time, rather than piping swirls, pipe haphazard wiggly lines all over the sheep.

Personalize the cake by using letter cutters to add a name, age and/or 'Happy Birthday' to the board.

Cup Cakes

Make cup cakes following the instructions on page 10. Cover the top of each cup cake with a disc of purple-blue sugarpaste. Using a no. 4 piping tube and three colours of buttercream, pipe on swirls and dots in the centre of the sugarpaste discs to create the sheep's bodies. Pipe the heads using the golden-brown buttercream, and smooth with a hot brush. Add ears and legs as for the main cake, using a no. 2 tube. Finally, add eyes and noses.

Cheeky Chimp

Here's a mischievous-looking chimp who would make a great party-table centrepiece. He has a broad grin and a twinkle in his eye, and looks full of fun. Use the carving template to form the base of his face, and then use sugarpaste to build up the features. His realistic-looking fur is simply made by marking the brown sugarpaste with a cutting tool and then painting over with paste colour. Invite him to any child's party, or make him for a fun-loving adult. Adorable chimp mini-cakes make perfect presents.

Materials

- 23cm (9in) chocolate round cake (see pages 8–9)
- 1 quantity buttercream
- sugarpaste (rolled fondant): 300g (11oz) white, 500g (1lb 2oz) dark brown, 500g (1lb 2oz) orange-beige
- gum tragacanth
- modelling paste: 15g (½oz) white, 25g (1oz) black
- sugar glue
- white vegetable fat (shortening)
- paste colour: dark brown (optional)
- clear spirit, such as gin or vodka (optional)

Although you can use water for painting paste colours onto sugarpaste, clear spirit, such as gin or vodka, will give the best results, as it is sterile and also evaporates quicker leaving the colour dry.

Equipment

- greaseproof paper
- cocktail sticks (toothpicks)
- boards: 23cm (9in) round cake board (not too thick as needs to be cut), 15cm (6in) round cake drum (board) (optional)
- waxed paper
- 5mm (³⁄₁₆in) spacers
- smoother
- palette knife
- Dresden tool
- cutting wheel
- craft knife
- ball tool
- narrow spacers made from 1.5mm (¹⁄₁₆in) thick card
- 3.5cm (1³⁄₈in) oval cutter
- sugar shaper with small round disc (optional)
- paintbrushes

Preparation

Preparing the head cake for freezing

Level the cake. Make a template from greaseproof paper and place on top of the cake. With a knife, cut vertically through the cake along the lines of the template (**A**). Insert cocktail sticks along the curved line between the mouth section and the eye section of the face (**B**). Remove the template carefully. Then, taking a large knife, reduce the height of the top of the face to 5cm (2in) by cutting horizontally up to the cocktail sticks (**C**). Remove the cocktail sticks and freeze the cake overnight.

Cutting the board

Place the template on top of the cake board and, using a pencil, trace around the outline, using the dashed lines in the chin area. Then cut out the face shape using a suitable sharp knife or a jigsaw.

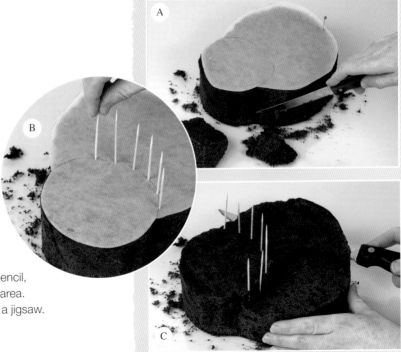

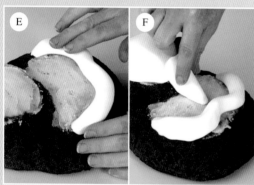

Stage One

Carving the cake

Remove the cake from the freezer then curve all the cut edges of the head and mouth area (**D**). Next, cut away a small wedge around the base of the mouth section to give a rounded appearance and so that the cake fits the cake board.

Covering the cake

1 Place the carved cake on top of the shaped board and place on waxed paper. Spread a thin layer of buttercream over the face area of the cake to stick the sugarpaste.

2 Create eyebrows by taking 100g (3½oz) white sugarpaste, rolling it into a sausage and then attaching it in place onto the front of the face, bringing the ends slightly down the sides of the face (**E**).

3 Make the mouth area more rounded by adding 150g (5oz) white sugarpaste to give extra height, then slightly slope the paste so that the chin area is higher than the nose. Finally, add a 40g (1½oz) cone-shaped piece of white sugarpaste onto the centre of the face for the nose, and smooth the sides (**F**).

4 Spread a thin layer of buttercream over the top and sides of the head. Knead the dark brown sugarpaste and roll out between the 5mm (³⁄₁₆in) spacers. Pick up the paste and place over the top section of the head. Smooth the paste around the sides of the cake and over the top of the eyebrows. Cut away the excess paste from the mouth and nose area. Take the smoother and, whilst pressing down, run the flat edge around the base of the cake to create a cutting line, and then cut away the excess paste with a palette knife (**G**).

5 Using a Dresden tool, mark a vertical line centrally over the back of the head. Take the cutting wheel and firstly mark guidelines onto the paste to indicate the direction in which the chimp's hair grows, that is, away from the parting and down the sides of the face. Then run it repeatedly over the surface of the paste to create hair texture, being careful not to cut right through the paste (**H**).

6 Spread a thin layer of buttercream over the remaining cake. Knead the orange-beige sugarpaste and roll it out between the 5mm (³⁄₁₆in) spacers. Pick up the paste and place over the mouth and eye section of the head. Carefully smooth the paste under the chin making sure there are no pleats. Cut the excess paste away from the base of the cake with a palette knife then, using a palette knife or craft knife, carefully remove the excess paste from around the face (**I**). Rub a finger over the cut edge to round it.

7 Take a palette knife and mark four short lines on the bridge of the nose, and then insert the small end of a ball tool into the end of the nose to form nostrils. Extend each nostril to the side by using the more rounded end of the Dresden tool (**J**).

Making modelling paste

Take 100g (3½oz) of the orange-beige sugarpaste trimmings and knead in 2.5ml (½ tsp) gum tragacanth to make modelling paste. Leave the paste to mature, ideally overnight.

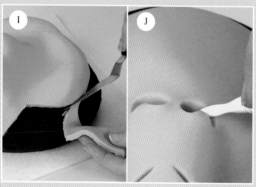

Stage Two

Eyes

1 Individually roll out the white and black modelling paste between the narrow spacers. Take the oval cutter and cut out two ovals of each colour. Carefully pick up the two white ovals and place vertically in position on the face. Reduce the height of the remaining black ovals by taking the oval cutter and making another cut (**K**).

2 Attach a foreshortened oval at the base of each eye to form the pupils. Make light spots by firstly cutting a 5mm (³/₁₆in) wide strip from thinly rolled white modelling paste, and then cut off two 2cm (¾in) lengths and curve them slightly. Attach to the eyes so that they lie partly over the pupil and partly over the whites.

Ears

1 Roll out the orange-beige modelling paste between the 5mm (³/₁₆in) spacers. Make an ear template from greaseproof paper and place it over the paste. Take a cutting wheel and cut around the template, then lightly roll the smaller wheel over the C-shaped line inside the ear. Remove the template and emphasise the C-shape marking with the sharper end of the Dresden tool (**L**).

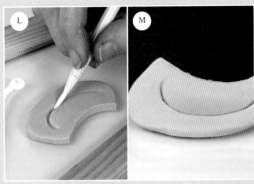

2 Paint some sugar glue along the inside edge of the ear and attach the ear to the side of the head, so that it partially rests against the side of the cake and partially against the waxed paper (**M**). Repeat for the second ear.

Mouth

1 Soften some black modelling paste. Do this by firstly kneading in some white vegetable fat to stop the paste becoming sticky and then partially dunk the paste into a small container of boiled water before kneading again (the paste should have the consistency of chewing gum). Place the softened paste with the small round disc into the sugar shaper and squeeze out a length. (Alternatively, you can roll a very thin piece of modelling paste for the mouth.) Take a fine paintbrush, and, using some sugar glue, paint a smile onto the mouth area of the cake.

2 Carefully pick up the length of black paste and place over the painted glue mouth, cut the ends to size with a craft knife. Paint on the corners of the mouth with sugar glue and add small lengths of black paste, again cutting them to size with a craft knife.

Finishing Touches (optional)

1 Once the ears have dried, place a little glue on top of the small cake drum and position the finished cake centrally on top – the cake drum allows the cake to be picked up and handled more easily.

2 Dilute some brown paste colour in clear spirit and paint over the top and sides of the chimp's head to highlight his hair (**N**).

❋ Animal Magic ❋

Add a baseball cap or brightly coloured hat or a flower, as for the mini-cakes.

❀

Position the cake on a large, square cake board and cover with pale-green sugarpaste, and then make a jungle scene with bright green leaves and bold, vivid flowers.

❀

Mini-cakes

Bake small half-ball-shaped cakes using the half-ball mini-cake pans (W) following instructions on page 11. Cover the cakes with buttercream and then build up the shape and cover with sugarpaste as for the main cake. Add mouths and eyes, and then personalize each cake as you like.

Squeak with Delight

Sophisticated, pink-cheeked little Matilda Mouse is smartly dressed up with matching hat, skirt and dainty handbag, all ready to go to a party. This adorable white mouse has a simply carved basic shape that is covered with sugarpaste. She is quite straightforward to create, and cut-out shapes make delightful and simple decorations. Matilda's loveable appearance would appeal to girls of all ages, and the stylish heart-shaped mini-cakes would be perfect to accompany her or to make as gifts.

Materials

- 20cm (8in) Madeira round cake (see pages 8–9)
- jam (optional)
- 1 quantity buttercream (plus extra if you wish to split and fill the cake)
- sugarpaste (rolled fondant): 1kg (2¼lb) deep purple (aubergine), 600g (1lb 5oz) white, 175g (6oz) lilac
- white vegetable fat (shortening)
- small amount of pastillage
- gum tragacanth
- sugar glue
- modelling paste: 50g (2oz) deep pink, 25g (1oz) peachy pink, 15g (½ oz) pale lilac, 10g (¼oz) black, 25g (1oz) mid pink
- 4mm (⅛in) silver dragées (sugar balls)

Equipment

- greaseproof paper
- 5mm (³/₁₆in) spacers
- 38cm (15in) round cake drum (board)
- smoother
- palette knife
- sugar shaper with small round, medium round and large round discs
- cocktail stick (toothpick)
- waxed paper
- Dresden tool
- narrow spacers made from 1.5mm (¹/₁₆in) thick card
- multisized ribbon cutter (optional)
- straightedge
- Elegant Heart cutters (LC): 4cm (1½in), 2.3cm (¹⁵/₁₆in), 1.5cm (⁹/₁₆in)
- craft knife
- circle cutters: 1.2cm (¹⁵/₃₂in), 2.5cm (1in)
- piping tubes (tips): nos 18 and 16, or small circle cutters
- 4cm (1½in) long petal cutter
- cutting wheel
- deep-pink ribbon and non-toxic glue stick
- wire flowers with glass centres (optional) (LC)

Preparation

Preparing the cake for freezing

Remove the crust from the cake, and then split and fill the cake with jam or buttercream, if you wish. Level the cake to a height of 6.5cm (2½in). Make the body and head templates from greaseproof paper and place on the cake. Cut vertically through the cake around both templates (**A**). Remove the templates. For the body, reduce the height of the neck to 3.5cm (1⅜in) by slicing up from the neck to the lower edge of the skirt (**B**). Freeze the cake overnight.

Covering the board

1 Roll out the deep-purple sugarpaste between the 5mm (³/₁₆in) spacers and use this to cover the board. (Rolling out the sugarpaste onto a surface smeared with white vegetable fat rather than icing (confectioners') sugar will ensure that there are no unwanted white marks on the paste.)

2 Smooth the paste level using a smoother. Trim the edges flush vertically with the sides of the board using a palette knife. Leave to dry.

Making whiskers

Soften the pastillage by kneading in some white vegetable fat and then partially dunking the paste into a small container of boiled water. Knead again. Place the paste with the small round disc into the sugar shaper. Squeeze out lengths (**C**). Straighten and leave to dry; an airing cupboard is an ideal place.

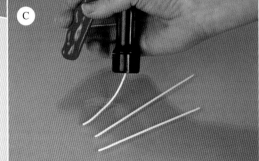

Stage One

Carving the cake

Remove the cake from the freezer. Curve the body side edges to give a rounded appearance to the skirt (**D**). Centrally place a cocktail stick 5cm (2in) from the top of the head; slice up from the point of the nose to the stick. Curve the head.

Covering the cake

1 Place the body cake on waxed paper and spread a thin layer of buttercream over the top only. Place some rolled white sugarpaste over the cake. Smooth to shape, using a smoother and your hand. Cut the paste flush with the base of the skirt. Place the smoother against one side of the body and run it along the side, to create a cutting line in the sugarpaste (**E**), repeat for the second side. Cut away the excess paste using a palette knife. Spread buttercream over the base of the skirt. Roll out the lilac sugarpaste and cut one edge straight. Place the straightedge against the base of the skirt, smooth and cut the paste flush with the top of the shirt (**F**).

2 Place the head cake on waxed paper and spread over a thin layer of buttercream. Cover the head with rolled white sugarpaste. Ease in the fullness of the paste around the top of the head, smooth and remove the excess. Leave to dry.

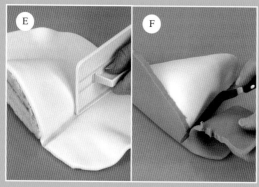

Making modelling paste

Take 50g (2oz) each of the lilac and white sugarpaste trimmings and knead in 1.5ml (¼ tsp) gum tragacanth to each to make modelling paste. Leave to mature.

Stage Two

Decorating the cake

Place the cake on the board, leaving room for the legs. Fill any gaps between the head and body with white sugarpaste. Smooth the joins with a Dresden tool.

Skirt

Roll out half of the lilac modelling paste between the narrow spacers and, using a multisized ribbon cutter (or a straightedge and a knife), cut out a 5cm (2in) wide strip. Paint sugar glue over the lower half of the body to stick the skirt in position (**G**). Ease in the fullness and cut off the excess with a palette knife.

Hat

Roll out the remaining lilac modelling paste between the narrow spacers and cut one edge straight. Paint sugar glue over the head where the hat will be placed. Place the paste over the glue so that the straight edge forms the rim of the hat. Ease in the fullness and cut away the excess.

Decorating the skirt and hat

1 Roll out the deep-pink modelling paste and cut into a 1.3cm (½in) wide strip using a multisized ribbon cutter or knife and straightedge. Place the largest heart cutter over the strip so that the widest end of the heart lies within the strip (**H**). Cut out several hearts. Paint a line of sugar glue over the lower edge of the skirt and attach the hearts around the hem of the skirt.

2 Repeat for the hat, cutting a 8mm (5/16in) wide strip and using the middle-sized heart. Soften some of the peachy pink modelling paste. Place the paste with the medium round disc into the sugar shaper. Paint glue around the lower edge of the skirt and the rim of the hat. Squeeze out two lengths of paste and place onto the glued lines. Cut to size using a craft knife. Glue a silver dragée in between each heart.

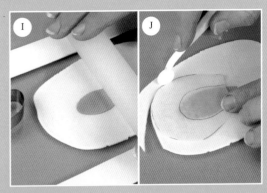

3 Soften some pale-lilac modelling paste, and place in the sugar shaper with the medium round disc. Paint a line of glue around the top of the skirt and attach a length of paste. Use the sharper end of a Dresden tool to create a pattern.

4 Thinly roll out the peachy pink and pale-lilac modelling pastes and cut out one large heart and seven medium hearts from the peachy pink and two 1.2cm ($^{15}/_{32}$in) circles and 8mm ($^{5}/_{16}$in) circles using the no. 18 tube from the pale lilac. Attach the larger heart with the larger circles either side to the front of the skirt and the smaller shapes in a pattern to the hat.

Legs, arms and tail

1 Place some softened white modelling paste with the large round disc into the sugar shaper. Paint lines of glue onto the cake and board for the legs, arms and tail. Attach five lengths of paste onto the glued lines. Cut to size using a craft knife. For the shoes, roll two 2cm (¾in) wide balls of deep-pink modelling paste, elongate each slightly and attach to the legs.

2 Roll two 1.2cm ($^{15}/_{32}$in) balls of white modelling paste, flatten slightly and then squeeze one end of each to form rounded triangle shapes. Take a pair of scissors and make two cuts into the wider end of each to form three fingers. Smooth the cut edges and attach the hands in place. Create a handbag using the modelling pastes and small cutters. Position in place.

Face and ear

1 Soften the black modelling paste and place in the sugar shaper with the small round disc. Paint a curved line of glue onto the face for the eye. Attach a length of paste to the glue, cut to size with a craft knife. Cut out a 2.5cm (1in) circle from thinly rolled mid-pink modelling paste and attach for the cheek. For the nose, roll a 2cm (¾in) ball from mid-pink modelling paste and attach.

2 Thinly roll out the mid-pink modelling paste and, using the petal cutter, cut out the inner ear. Roll out the white modelling paste between the narrow spacers. Place the inner ear onto the white and roll the pastes together (**I**). Place the ear template on top so that the inner ear on the template corresponds to the pink area of paste, and cut around the template with a cutting wheel (**J**).

3 Lift half up and support with kitchen paper (**K**). When partially dry, position it, supporting with kitchen paper (**L**).

Finishing touches

Using a non-toxic glue stick attach the ribbon around the sides of the board to complete the cake. Scatter wire flowers over the board to decorate, if you like.

Mini Cakes

Bake heart-shaped mini- and bitesized cakes using the Heart Minicake and Petite Heart Pans (W), following instructions on page 11. Cover the cakes with buttercream and then deep-purple sugarpaste. Decorate the cakes as for the main cake.

❋ Animal Magic ❋

Personalize the mouse by dressing it in the recipient's favourite colours.

❀

If you need to feed a large number of guests you could bake a large slab cake and then place the mouse cake on top.

❀

Use letter cutters to add a name, age and/or 'Happy Birthday' to the space on the board.

Vamp It Up!

No Hallowe'en is complete without a few bats, so if you don't have any in your belfry, make this far-from-frightening vampire bat to invite to your Hallowe'en festivities. Flying in a glittering, star-lit sky, this spooky bat has amazing wings made by laying modelling paste over a pastillage structure. The cake is baked in a ball tin and then simply covered with sugarpaste. Ideal for an adults' or children's party – make sure your celebration is complete with this bat and his accompanying pumpkin lantern, bat and ghostly cookies.

Materials

- 100g (3½oz) black pastillage
- white vegetable fat (shortening)
- sugar glue
- modelling paste: 175g (6oz) black, 15g (½oz) white
- sugarpaste (rolled fondant): 900g (2lb) purple-blue, 600g (1lb 5oz) black
- icing (confectioners') sugar (optional)
- 13cm (5in) chocolate ball cake (see pages 8–9)
- 1 quantity buttercream
- peacock sparkle dust

Equipment

- plastic sleeves
- sugar shaper with large round and medium round discs
- craft knife
- Plasticine or modelling clay
- narrow spacers made from 1.5mm (¹⁄₁₆in) thick card
- cutting wheel
- 5mm (³⁄₁₆in) spacers
- 35.5 × 30cm (14 × 12in) oval cake drum (board)
- smoother
- palette knife
- waxed paper
- small scissors
- card
- dowel
- circle cutters: 3.5cm (1³⁄₈in), 1cm (³⁄₈in)
- no. 17 piping tube (tip)
- Dresden tool
- soft paintbrush
- star cutters (LC)
- blue ribbon and non-toxic glue stick

Preparation

Wing structures

1 Trace two wing outline templates and place inside plastic sleeves with one template the reverse of the other. Soften the pastillage. Do this by firstly kneading in some white vegetable fat to stop the paste becoming sticky and then partially dunking the paste into a small container of boiled water before kneading again (the paste should have the consistency of chewing gum). Place the softened paste with the large round disc into the sugar shaper. Squeeze out lengths onto the templates (**A**). Stick the paste with sugar glue at the join, straighten each section and cut to size with a craft knife. Leave to dry thoroughly; an airing cupboard is an ideal place.

2 Once the pastillage is dry, take some Plasticene or modelling clay and roll it into four cones to fit between the two outer sections of each wing (see picture B). Cover each cone with clear film (plastic wrap). Place the wings on a level surface (remember: one should be a mirror image of the other), and position the cones. Paint a line of sugar glue along the three outer sections (**B**).

3 Take some of the black modelling paste and roll it out between the narrow spacers. Place the outer wing template on top of the paste and cut around it with a cutting wheel. Pick up the paste and place it onto the glued supports of the wing so that it rests on the cones (**C**). Turn the template over and cut out the second outer wing section, as before, then position on the other wing. Leave to one side to dry.

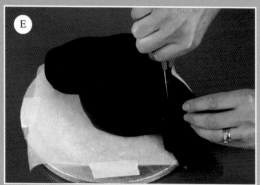

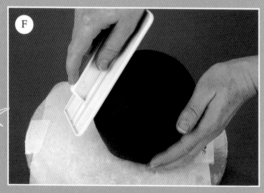

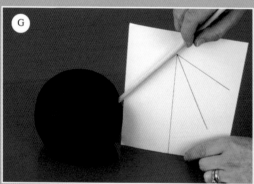

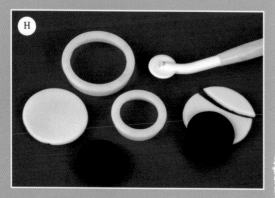

Covering the board

Knead the purple-blue sugarpaste until warm. Then roll out between the 5mm (³/₁₆in) spacers using icing sugar or white vegetable fat to prevent sticking. Lift up the paste, using a rolling pin for support, and place it over the board. Take a smoother and, using a circular motion, smooth the paste to give a level surface. Using a palette knife, trim the edges flush with the sides of the board, taking care to keep the cut vertical. Place to one side to dry.

Stage One

Covering the cake

1 Level the two halves of the cake in line with the top of the tins, and then stick the two halves together with buttercream to create a ball cake.

2 Place the cake on waxed paper and spread a thin layer of buttercream over it to stick the sugarpaste. Knead the black sugarpaste to warm it, then roll it out. Pick up the paste and carefully place it over the cake so that the paste meets the base of one side of the ball and goes over the top to the base on the other side (**D**). Encourage the excess paste into two pleats on opposite sides of the ball, where the wings will be situated. Take a sharp pair of scissors and cut away the pleats so that the sugarpaste is flush with the cake (**E**).

3 Using a combination of a smoother and the palm of your hand, smooth the sugarpaste to blend the joins (**F**). As long as you keep working the paste it will remain pliable; the joins should completely disappear, but don't worry if they are being stubborn, as the wings should cover most of them. Place to one side to dry.

Stage Two

Decorating the cake

Transfer the wing outline template onto card, excluding the dotted section. Place the card up against one side of the cake and insert the dowel into the cake at the same angle at the top of the wing (**G**). Remove the dowel and repeat for the second wing. Carefully transfer the cake to the covered board, placing the ball in the centre of the board but slightly towards the back.

Ears Roll some black modelling paste between the narrow spacers. Place the ear template over the paste and cut around it with a cutting wheel. Paint a line of glue on one side of the top of the head and attach the ear in position. Repeat for the second ear, remembering to turn the template over.

Eyes Individually roll out some of the white and black modelling paste. Cut two 3.5cm (1³/₈in) white circles from the white modelling paste and two 1cm (³/₈in) from the black modelling paste. Place the black circles on top of the white (**H**), so that they overlap the edges of the white, and then cut away the excess with the 3.5cm (1³/₈in) cutter. Shape the upper edge of the white of the eye with a cutting wheel, remembering that the eyes should be mirror images of each other. Cut a small dot using the no. 17 piping tube and add to the top of each pupil for a light spot. Attach in place on the cake using sugar glue.

Wings Carefully insert the wings into the holes made earlier so that the lowest section of the wing rests on the board. Roll out the remaining black modelling paste between the narrow spacers and place the inner wing template on the paste. Cut around the template with a cutting wheel. Paint lines of glue along the wing structure at the back of the uncovered section and 4cm (1½in) down the side of the cake, below the top of the wing. Position the paste so that it fits, encouraging the fullness to the back of the wing (**I**). Use a Dresden tool to blend the edge of the wing into the bat's body. Repeat for the second wing.

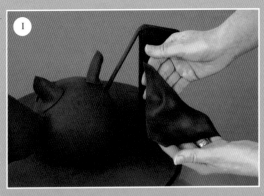

Mouth and eyebrows Soften some of the black modelling paste. Do this by firstly kneading in some white vegetable fat to stop the paste becoming sticky and then partially dunking the paste into a small container of boiled water before kneading again (the paste should have the consistency of chewing gum). Place the softened paste with the medium round disc into the sugar shaper. Paint a line of glue onto the cake for the mouth, and lines above the eyes for eyebrows. Squeeze out one long and two short lengths of paste from the sugar shaper and place onto the glued lines.

Decorating the board
Take the soft paintbrush and the sparkle dust, and liberally dust the board (**J**). Roll out the white modelling paste between the narrow spacers and cut out a selection of stars (**K**). Attach randomly to the board using sugar glue.

Finishing touches
Using a non-toxic glue stick attach the ribbon around the sides of the board to complete the cake.

Cookies
Using Hallowe'en cookie cutters, make the cookies as described on page 12, (Wilton Hallowe'en cutter set is ideal). Decorate the cookies as desired using thinly rolled modelling paste.

Animal Magic

Change the expression to make a gleeful bat.

❀

Add purple lustre dusts to the wings.

❀

Make additional stars for candleholders to add to the board.

❀

Personalize the cake by using letter cutters to add a name, age and/or 'Happy Birthday' to the board.

Whale of a Time

Emerging from the frothy waves of the blue ocean comes this adorable whale, spraying water and ready to greet her party guests with a huge smile. The subtle markings on her body are achieved by stippling two shades of blue over the sugarpaste, and the sea is an opportunity for you to create superbly realistic waves from marbled sugarpaste painted with royal icing and piping gel. Appealing to many ages, but perfect for the under fives, this whale cake is accompanied by painted dolphin cookies.

Materials

- ❀ 20 × 30cm (8 × 12in) chocolate cake (see pages 8–9)
- ❀ 1 quantity buttercream
- ❀ modelling paste: 50g (2oz) white, 115g (4oz) slate blue, 15g (½ oz) black
- ❀ white vegetable fat (shortening)
- ❀ sugar glue

- ❀ sugarpaste (rolled fondant): 1.3kg (2lb 14oz) slate blue, 800g (1¾lb) in six shades of blue
- ❀ paste colour: blue, purple-blue
- ❀ clear spirit, such as gin or vodka
- ❀ small amount of royal icing
- ❀ edible white sparkle/lustre dust (SK – Frost)
- ❀ confectioners' glaze
- ❀ piping gel

Equipment

- ❀ greaseproof paper
- ❀ glass-headed dressmakers' pins
- ❀ 24-gauge metallic silver floristry wires
- ❀ cocktail sticks (toothpicks)
- ❀ 40.5 × 35.5cm (16 ×14in) oval cake drum (board)
- ❀ 5mm (³/₁₆in) spacers
- ❀ palette knife
- ❀ smoother
- ❀ craft knife

- ❀ stippling brush
- ❀ paintbrushes
- ❀ narrow spacers made from 1.5mm (¹/₁₆in) thick card
- ❀ no. 18 piping tube (tip)
- ❀ sugar shaper with small round disc
- ❀ posy pick
- ❀ oasis fix
- ❀ blue sparkly ribbon and non-toxic glue stick

Preparation

Preparing the head cake for freezing

1 Level the cake and cut in half to make two 20 × 15cm (8 × 6in) cakes. Spread buttercream over the top of one cake and stack the second on top. Make outline and profile templates from greaseproof paper and place the outline template on top of the cake. Cut vertically around the template (**A**). Place the profile template onto one side of the cake using dressmakers' pins.

2 Holding the knife horizontally, cut away the cake along the outline of the template (**B**). Freeze the cake overnight.

Water spray

1 Warm the white modelling paste by kneading it and adding white vegetable fat and boiled water as necessary. Roll a marble-sized ball of paste in your hand to eliminate any cracks. Roll the ball backwards and forwards until it becomes a cone. Dip one end of a floristry wire into the sugar glue and insert it into the pointed end of the cone. Roll the paste on the wire between your fingers to lengthen the cone slightly. Make 12 more.

2 Roll several pea-sized balls of white modelling paste. Insert floristry wires through some so that the balls are 5cm (2in) from the end of the wires. Top each wire with a ball.

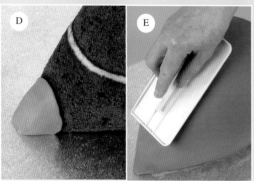

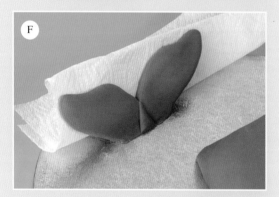

Stage One

Carving the cake

1 Remove the cake from the freezer. Insert cocktail sticks in a central line over the top of the cake. Cut from the top central line towards the central buttercream line using a curved cut (**C**).

2 Remove a curved wedge of cake from below the horizontal buttercream line all the way around the cake.

Covering the cake

1 Place the cake on the cake drum, leaving room for a tail. Add a small amount of the slate-blue sugarpaste to shape the back of the body (**D**). Spread a thin layer of buttercream over the cake to stick the sugarpaste. Roll out the slate-blue sugarpaste between the 5mm (³/₁₆in) spacers. Place the paste over the cake. Ease in the fullness around the front, bringing the excess towards the back and ease it in; try to avoid creating any pleats. Cut away the excess paste around the base.

2 Smooth the sugarpaste using a smoother and the palm of your hand (**E**). The paste will remain pliable while you work, so spend time perfecting the finish. Leave to dry.

Tail

Roll out the slate-blue modelling paste between the 5mm (³/₁₆in) spacers. Cut around the tail template on the paste with a craft knife. Smooth the cut edge with a finger. Add a small triangle of paste to the centre of the tail, and attach to the board at an angle of 45 degrees. Support with kitchen paper while it dries (**F**).

Stage Two

Painting the cake

Separately dilute some blue and purple-blue paste colours in clear spirit. Stipple the purple-blue paste colour over the top of the whale and partially down the sides with the stippling brush (**G**). Change to the blue, and stipple the middle of each side. Then dilute the purple-blue a little more and paint the underside of the whale. Paint the tail in the same way. Leave to dry.

Stage Three

Decorating the board – the waves

1 Knead the six shades of blue sugarpaste to warm it. Break the coloured pastes into small pieces and scatter them over your work surface to mix up the colours. Gather the pieces together into a ball and briefly knead together. Cut across the ball to reveal the marbled pattern. Place the two half-balls next to one another and then roll the paste out between the 5mm (³/₁₆in) spacers using white vegetable fat to prevent sticking (**H**). Alter the rolling direction as the pattern develops to get the best effect.

2 Roll long sausages of sugarpaste trimmings. Paint lines of sugar glue onto the board at right angles to the direction in which the waves are travelling. Add the sausages to the board to give height to the waves.

3 Cut away a section of the marbled sugarpaste and place over the wave formers (**I**). With a finger, mould and stroke the paste to form wave shapes (**J**). Trim away the excess paste from the edge of the board.

4 Cut another section of the rolled-out sugarpaste and place onto the board, abutting it with the first. Blend the join with the heat of a finger and then shape the waves as before.

5 Using a paintbrush, apply white royal icing to the tips of the waves to make surf. Take a damp flat-headed brush and drag the royal icing back over the tops of the waves for a realistic finish (**K**).

Eyes

Roll out white and black modelling pastes between the narrow spacers. Using the no. 18 piping tube and the white paste, cut out two large circles using the wider end of the tube and two small circles using the smaller end. Cut two large circles from the black. Flatten the larger white circles by pressing down with a smoother. Place the large white circles in place for eyes, then add the black pupils and the smaller white circle for a light spot.

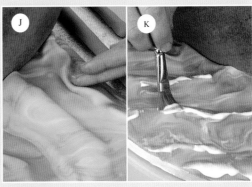

Smile

Soften some black modelling paste, place with the small round disc into the sugar shaper and squeeze out a length. Use a fine paintbrush to paint a smile in sugar glue onto the cake. Place the length of black paste over the glue mouth; cut to size with a craft knife. Paint on the corners of the mouth and add small lengths of black paste, cut to fit.

Water spray

1 Using a paintbrush, cover each of the dried water droplets with white vegetable fat. Using a soft brush, cover each droplet with the edible sparkle/lustre dust (**L**). Insert the posy pick into the top of the cake just below the surface of the paste.

2 Insert a small sausage of oasis fix to keep the wires in place. Take a wired droplet and gently curve the wire by wrapping it around a cylinder such as a food can. Cut the wire into an appropriate length and insert into the posy pick. Create the basic shape of the spray by arranging some curved wired water droplets of the same length to form the lower part of the spray. Take the straight wires with the round droplets and place these in the centre to define the height. Bend the lower ones out slightly. Fill the spaces with the remaining droplets.

Finishing touches

Paint over the sugarpaste waves with confectioners' glaze to seal them. Mix some of the sparkle dust with the glaze and add to the back of the waves. Paint over the sea with piping gel to make it reflective. Using a non-toxic glue stick, attach the ribbon around the sides of the board to complete the cake.

Cookies

Using dolphin cookie cutters, make the cookies as described on page 12. Decorate the cookies using water icing coloured in white and a selection of blues.

Animal Magic

Add candles to the waves.

❧

Pipe a message onto the side of the whale, such as 'Bon Voyage' for a special cake for someone who is moving overseas.

❧

Use bright colours to make a 'funky' whale.

❧

Personalize the cake by using letter cutters to add a name, age and/or 'Happy Birthday' to the board.

❧

Roaring Success

Here's a tiger that is truly burning bright and would make a stunning centrepiece for a child's or adult's party. Sculpted chocolate cake is covered with sugarpaste and then painted with edible paste colours. This is an opportunity for you to display your painting talents, but the effect is surprisingly straightforward to create by following the step-by-step instructions. Allow plenty of time to carve the head while the cake is frozen to achieve a realistic form. Make 'furry' or mini-tiger cup cakes to complete the theme.

Materials

- ✿ two 23cm (9in) round chocolate cakes (see pages 8–9)
- ✿ 2 quantities white chocolate buttercream
- ✿ white unbreakable gel (OP)
- ✿ confectioners' glaze
- ✿ sugarpaste (rolled fondant): 1.2kg (2lb 10oz) white
- ✿ gum tragacanth
- ✿ sugar glue
- ✿ modelling paste: 25g (1oz) olive, 15g (½oz) black
- ✿ white vegetable fat (shortening)
- ✿ paste colours: golden brown (Spectral-Autumn Leaf), black, pink
- ✿ clear spirit, such as gin or vodka
- ✿ piping gel

Equipment

- ✿ greaseproof paper
- ✿ glass-headed dressmakers' pins
- ✿ piping tubes (tips): nos 2 and 16 (optional)
- ✿ plastic sheet
- ✿ cake drums (boards): 15cm (6in), 23cm (9in) round
- ✿ 5mm (³/₁₆in) spacers
- ✿ palette knife
- ✿ cutting wheel
- ✿ ball tool
- ✿ Dresden tool
- ✿ pan scourer
- ✿ cocktail stick (toothpick)
- ✿ craft knife
- ✿ oval cutters: 6.5cm (2½in) (FMM), 1.5cm (⁹/₁₆in)
- ✿ fine and soft paintbrushes
- ✿ sugar shaper with small ribbon disc (optional)
- ✿ sharp scissors

Preparation

Preparing the cake for freezing

1 Level the cakes, spread a layer of buttercream on top of one and stack the other on top. Make two profile templates from greaseproof paper and, using glass-headed dressmakers' pins, attach to the sides of the stacked cakes so that one is positioned as a mirror image to the other. With one template facing you hold a large carving knife with the blade reaching from one template to the other and cut the cake to form the tiger's profile (**A**).

2 Make a face template from greaseproof paper and attach to the top of the cake so that the tip of the muzzle is in line with the muzzle of the carved cake. Roughly carve away the cake from the muzzle and eye sockets (**B**). Freeze the cake overnight.

Whiskers

1 Mix the unbreakable gel by following the instructions on the packet. Let the mixture stand for at least 4 hours to mature, then, using the no. 2 tube, pipe straight lines onto a plastic sheet and leave to dry (**C**).

Use up all the mixed gel to make lines so that you will have a few spare.

2 Once dry, paint each whisker with confectioners' glaze to prevent the whiskers being affected by moisture and then drooping.

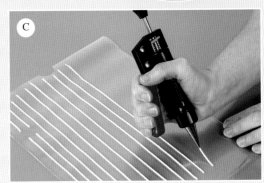

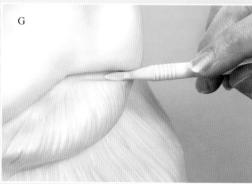

Stage One

Carving the cake

Having a 3-D model of a tiger, cat or dog such as a Labrador for reference will help you achieve the basic shape.

1 Remove the cake from the freezer. Carve the cut edges of the muzzle to create a more rounded appearance. With a small knife carefully cut out the nostrils (**D**) and the mouth (**E**).

2 Slope the back and sides of the head and cut away a small area of cake between the eyebrows. Next, cut a shallow wedge of cake vertically away from the back of the head. Adjust the shape of the eye area as necessary.

Covering the cake

1 The cake is covered in three sections. Attach the 15cm (6in) cake drum centrally under the 23cm (9in) cake drum. Place the cake on top of the stacked cake drums and spread a thin layer of buttercream over the cake to stick the sugarpaste.

2 If necessary, adjust the shape of the muzzle, eyebrows, and so on, by adding pieces of sugarpaste to change the overall shape slightly.

Chin

1 Roll out some of the white sugarpaste between the 5mm ($^3/_{16}$in) spacers and place the paste under the chin of the tiger so that it covers the lower lip and comes partly around the sides of the face and over the edges of the cake drum. Remove the excess paste from the base by holding a palette knife under the 23cm (9in) drum and cutting through the paste.

2 Take the cutting wheel and mark guidelines onto the paste to indicate the direction in which the fur grows.

3 Run it repeatedly over the surface of the paste to create a fur texture, being careful not to cut right through the paste.

Vary the length of the stroke and shape of the cuts to create realistic fur.

Back of the head

Roll some white sugarpaste and use to cover the top, sides and back of the head. Add texture using the cutting wheel.

Muzzle

1 Roll out the remaining sugarpaste and use to cover the muzzle. Cut away the excess paste and blend the joins with the heat of a finger.

2 Insert the larger end of a ball tool into each nostril and circle to shape (**F**), then, using a finger, smooth the top outer part of each nostril back and up towards the eyes.

3 Take a Dresden tool and indent the line of the mouth (**G**), the line around the nose and the vertical line joining the nose and mouth (see picture H). Next, take a pan scourer, and firmly press it into the paste either side and on top of the muzzle to create a subtle texture (**H**).

4 Texture all the remaining fur with the cutting wheel (**I**), then make small indents around the nose especially around the outer indented corners. Finally, take a cocktail stick and indent four rows of holes for whiskers on either side of the face (**J**). Leave to dry.

Making white modelling paste

Take 100g (3½oz) of the white sugarpaste trimmings and knead in 2.5ml (½ tsp) of gum tragacanth to make modelling paste. Leave the modelling paste to mature, ideally overnight.

If you are pushed for time, use CMC instead of gum tragacanth, as it reacts much quicker.

Stage Two

Adding the ears

1 Knead the white modelling paste until warm then roll out between the 5mm (³/16in) spacers.

If your modelling paste is dry and crumbly, add some white fat and boiled water, and knead well.

2 Make an ear template from greaseproof paper and place it over the paste. Take a craft knife and cut around the template, then texture with a cutting wheel using vertical strokes and cutting through the edges of the paste to give a slightly ragged appearance (**K**). Turn the ear over and texture the back.

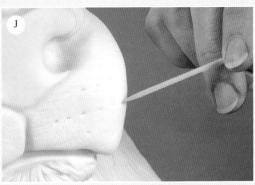

3 Paint sugar glue along the base of the ear and place on the head, supporting the paste in position with cocktail sticks while the paste dries (see picture L). Blend the base of the ear into the head using a Dresden tool and then, as far as possible, texture the join with a cutting wheel.

4 Turn the ear template and cut out a mirror image of the first ear; texture and position as before.

5 Roll out some of the remaining modelling paste into a thin strip, and, using a cutting wheel, make parallel cuts by rolling the wheel from the centre of the paste to the outside to give a jagged appearance (see picture M). Using a palette knife cut across these cuts and attach the resulting strips to the base of the ears. Support in position with kitchen paper (**L**).

6 Thinly roll out some white modelling paste and, using the 6.5cm (2½in) oval cutter, cut out two ovals. Texture each, by running the cutting wheel from one of the narrow ends of the oval to give a fan effect, cutting through the edges of the paste to give a ragged appearance as before (**M**). Paint sugar glue onto the inside top edges of the inner ears and position the textured ovals so that about two-thirds of the oval extends into the ear. Cut away the excess paste at the back of the ear and blend the join.

If you have a dog or cat, look at the direction its fur grows around its face.

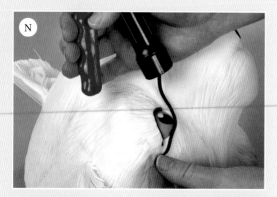

Adding the eyes

1 Knead the olive modelling paste until warm then roll into a ball, cut the ball in half and roll each half into a 2.5cm (1in) diameter ball. Place the eyeball centrally into the eye socket and flatten slightly.

2 For pupils, thinly roll out the black modelling paste and cut out two small ovals using the 1.5cm (9/16in) cutters. Attach these to the centre of the eyes.

3 For the light spots, thinly roll out some white modelling paste and cut out two small circles using the no.16 piping tube. Alternatively, roll small balls of white paste, then attach them in the same position on each eye.

4 To create the eyelids, roll four balls of white sugarpaste and elongate each into a sausage. Wrap one sausage around half of an eyeball, then, using a finger, blend and shape the paste. Texture the paste with a cutting wheel and then define the inner edge of the eyelid with a Dresden tool. Repeat for the other three sausages. Create indents for the tear ducts with a Dresden tool.

Black detail

Take a fine paintbrush, and, using some sugar glue, paint the inner edges of the eyelids, top of the nose and inside of the mouth. Soften some black modelling paste. Do this by firstly kneading in some white vegetable fat to stop the paste getting sticky and then partially dunk the paste into a small container of boiled water before kneading again (the paste should have the consistency of chewing gum). Place the softened paste with the small ribbon disc into the sugar shaper, and squeeze out some lengths. Alternatively, roll the paste thinly by hand. Carefully pick up a length of black paste and place over one section of inner eyelid (**N**). Cut the ends to size with a craft knife. Repeat for the other eyelids, the nose and mouth (**O**).

Stage Three

Painting the cake

1 Dilute some golden-brown paste colour with clear spirit and, using a large, soft paintbrush, start to apply to the cake (**P**) using the pictures opposite as a guide. (Save time by painting over the whole of the brown area rather than leaving white patches for the black stripes, if you like.)

2 Where the brown merges into the white, dilute the paste colour so that the transition is gradual. Dilute some pink paste colour and paint the nose. Dilute the black paste colour just enough to make it into a painting consistency. Using a range of soft brushes, apply the distinctive tiger's markings over the top of the painted cake. Finally, using a fine paintbrush and some golden-brown paste colour add some radial strokes to the iris of each eye (see picture Q).

Painting tips

Although tackling a complicated painting project might seem daunting at first, you can achieve great results if you work carefully.

❀ Painting is easier if you have the right tools, so invest in good-quality paintbrushes.

❀ Ensure the first painted layer is completely dry before painting the next layer to avoid accidentally taking off the paint.

❀ Try to avoid making the black paste colour too thin, otherwise it may run.

❀ If you make a mistake with your painting you can carefully remove a small area with a dampened flat-headed paintbrush.

❀ Work slowly and stop every so often to stand back and check how the painting looks.

Don't worry too much about copying the markings exactly, invent your own; tiger markings tend not to be symmetrical so slight variations are fine.

Finishing touches

Eyes Firstly, paint over the eyes with some confectioner's glaze to seal the painted surface, and then warm some piping gel in a microwave or a heatproof bowl over a pan of simmering water until the gel is lump-free. Load a paintbrush and carefully add enough gel to the tiger's eyes to cover them completely (**Q**).

Whiskers Insert the whiskers into the holes made earlier in the muzzle and trim them using a small pair of scissors. Also add two whiskers to the top of each eyebrow (**R**).

Animal Magic

Omit the whiskers and glazing for the eyes, to make a quicker cake.

❁

Alter the markings to make a jaguar, cheetah, puma or leopard, using a picture as a reference.

❁

Copy a picture of a Siamese cat or loved moggy or make a dog such as a golden retriever or Labrador. Just change the ears and whiskers; the shapes are very similar.

Cup Cakes

Make the cup cakes following the instructions on page 10. Cover the top of each cup cake with a disc of white sugarpaste, if making the fur effect, or use a coloured sugarpaste. To make tiger's fur, texture the white sugarpaste using a cutting wheel and paint as for the main cake. To create the tiger's head, make a mould as shown on page 13 using Plasticine or modelling clay and moulding gel, then, using white modelling paste and the mould, make tiger's heads. Paint as for the main cake and attach to the top of the cup cakes.

Tall Story

With his head reaching up into the leaves of a tree, this giraffe is pictured on a hot African savanna. His eye-catching spotted coat and friendly face make him fun to make, and his markings are surprisingly simple to accomplish by painting paste colours onto geometric shapes of modelling paste. Careful sculpting of the body and head are essential for the perfect finished result, so take time with these. Any child would love to invite this giraffe to their birthday party, and there are fun mini-cakes to go with him as well.

Materials

- 20cm (8in) round Madeira cake (see pages 8–9)
- jam (optional)
- 1 quantity buttercream (plus extra if you wish to split and fill the cake)
- sugarpaste (rolled fondant): 1kg (2¼lb) light cream
- icing (confectioners') sugar (optional)
- white vegetable fat (shortening)
- paste colours: cream, golden brown (Spectral – Autumn Leaf), brown, olive green
- clear spirit, such as gin or vodka
- gum tragacanth
- sugar glue
- modelling paste: 25g (1oz) green

Equipment

- greaseproof paper
- glass-headed dressmakers' pins
- 5mm (³/₁₆in) spacers
- 40.5 × 35.5cm (16 × 14in) oval cake drum (board)
- smoother
- palette knife
- paintbrushes, including a large flat-headed one
- turntable (optional)
- cocktail stick (toothpick)
- scriber (optional)
- narrow spacers made from 1.5mm (¹/₁₆in) thick card
- craft knife
- cutting wheel
- no. 1.5 piping tube (tip)
- sugar shaper
- oval cutters (K): 1.6cm (⁵/₈in), 7mm (⁹/₃₂in)
- paisley cutters (LC) or leaf cutters
- olive green ribbon and non-toxic glue stick

Preparation

Preparing the head cake for freezing

Level the cake to a height of 6.5cm (2½in), then, if you wish, split and fill the cake with layers of jam and buttercream. Make head and body templates from greaseproof paper and place on top of the levelled cake. Roughly cut away the head section and reduce the height of this section to 5cm (2in). With a knife, cut vertically around both templates (**A**). Freeze the cake overnight.

Covering the board

Knead the light-cream sugarpaste until warm. Then roll it out between the 5mm (³/₁₆in) spacers using icing sugar or white vegetable fat to prevent sticking. Lift up the paste, using a rolling pin for support, and place it over the board. Take a smoother and, using a circular motion, smooth the paste to give a level surface. Using a palette knife, trim the edges flush with the sides of the board, taking care to keep the cut vertical. Place to one side to dry.

Painting the board

1 Separately mix the cream and golden-brown paste colours with clear spirit or boiled water. Then, using a large flat-headed paintbrush apply to the board in sweeping strokes. Start with the cream at one end of the oval board (**B**) and gradually increase the depth of colour as you work down the board. Stop halfway and change to the golden-brown colour. Starting with a strong colour at the base, apply strokes of colour in decreasing strengths over the lower half of the board (**C**). Blend the colours using a damp brush.

To adjust, blend or remove colour, paint over the area with a clean, damp brush.

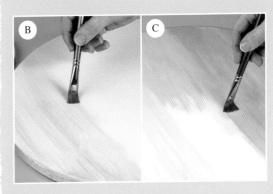

D

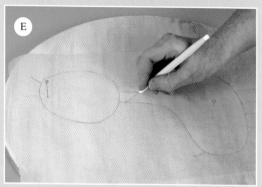

E

F

G

H

2 Place the board on a turntable or the edge of your work surface and, with a paintbrush, carefully paint the sides of the sugarpaste board to match the colour above (this is to give a neat finish when the ribbon is added). The colour of the board can be lightened when dry by using some damp kitchen paper and carefully wiping away a little colour using a circular action.

Stage One

Carving the cake

1 Remove the cake from the freezer. For the body, place the knife on the neck 2cm (¾in) above the base of the cake, and then carefully make a sloping cut up to the body. Curve all the top edges of the cake to give a rounded appearance (see picture D) and then cut away a small triangle from around the base of the cake to shape the underneath.

2 For the head, centrally place a cocktail stick 2.5cm (1in) in from the lower, wider, edge of the head. Place the knife at the top of the head 2cm (¾in) above the base of the cake, then make a curved cut up to the cocktail stick. Make a similar cut 2cm (¾in) up from the lower section of the head to the cocktail stick. Then curve all the top edges to give a rounded appearance to the cake. Next, cut away a small triangle from around the base of the cake (D).

When carving an animal shape remember to curve the underneath of the body to form a rounded belly. This will give a realistic shape. During carving stand back every so often so that you can see the shape from a little further away, and look at its profile to check that it is taking shape correctly.

Covering the cake

1 Trace the giraffe template onto greaseproof paper and place onto the prepared board using glass-headed dressmakers' pins to secure. Take a scriber or pin and scribe around the giraffe's outline, the lines that mark the position of the horns, legs and tail and the outline of the feet (E).

2 Place the head cake in place on the board and carefully spread over a thin layer of buttercream. Brush away any excess crumbs. Knead the cream sugarpaste until warm then roll out between the 5mm (³/₁₆in) spacers and place over the cake (F). Ease in the fullness of paste around the sides of the cake. Smooth the paste firstly with a smoother and then the heat of your hand to create an even surface. Take the smoother and, while pressing down, run the flat edge around the base of the cake to create a cutting line (G). Cut away the excess paste with a palette knife (H).

3 Place the body cake within the scribed area on the board. Roll a small ball of sugarpaste into a cone and place between the head and body cake to extend the neck. Smooth to shape with a finger (I).

4 Spread a thin layer of buttercream over the body cake and carefully brush away any excess crumbs. Roll out the remaining sugarpaste and cut one edge straight. Place the cut edge against the head and ease the paste over the body. Smooth the cake, then run a smoother around the base of the body and neck as far as possible to create a cutting line. Cut away the excess with a palette knife and place to one side to dry.

Making modelling paste

Take 150g (5oz) of sugarpaste trimmings and knead in 2.5ml (½ tsp) gum tragacanth to make modelling paste. Remove 50g (2oz) and colour it a deep golden brown. Leave the pastes to mature, ideally overnight.

Stage Two

Decorating the cake

1 For the spots, knead the golden-brown modelling paste until warm, adding a little white vegetable fat and boiled water if necessary to make the paste elastic and workable, then roll out between the narrow spacers. Take a craft knife and cut irregularly shaped pentagons in the paste, positioning them so that they roughly fit together (**J**). Lift the excess paste away from the pentagons (**K**) and stick the shapes to the body of the giraffe with sugar glue.

2 For the horns, roll some cream modelling paste into a 7mm (⁹/₃₂in) wide sausage shape. Cut the sausage into two 2cm (¾in) lengths and attach to the top of the head with sugar glue. Roll two pea-sized balls of golden-brown modelling paste and attach one to the end of each sausage.

To achieve an even sausage, you may find it easier to roll the paste to size with a smoother.

3 Thinly roll out some of the golden-brown modelling paste and cut one edge straight. Take a cutting wheel and make close 1cm (³/₈in) deep cuts at right angles to the cut edge for about 4cm (1½in). Cut a line across the base of the cuts then cut the textured strip in half. Wrap the resulting textured strips around the top of each ball to complete the top of the horns.

To make balls of equal sizes roll a larger ball and cut it in half.

4 For the tail, roll a small amount of cream modelling paste into a ball and then a cone, and position onto the scribed line. Secure in place with sugar glue.

5 For the mane, roll out the golden-brown modelling paste into a strip and cut into it with a cutting wheel to a depth of 1.5cm (⁹/₁₆in) as for the horns. Cut across the base and attach the resulting strip to the left of the neck using sugar glue. Add a few tufts of textured paste between the horns and to the tip of the tail.

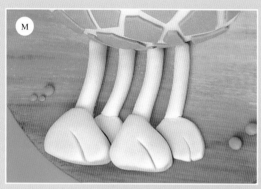

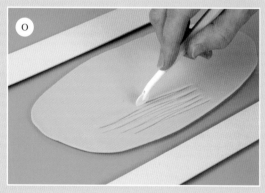

6 For the ears, make an ear template then roll out some cream modelling paste between the narrow spacers and cut out two ears, remembering to turn the template over for the second ear. Attach the ears to the head using sugar glue. Lift up the edges of each ear and prop up with kitchen paper to give the ears more character (**L**).

7 For the legs, roll a 9cm (3½in) long 1.25cm (½in) wide sausage from cream sugarpaste. Cut it in half and place over the scribed lines of the giraffe's right hind leg and right front leg. Secure in place with sugar glue. Roll another sausage of the same length but this time only 8mm (⁵⁄₁₆in) wide. Cut in half and position over the scribed lines of the left legs.

8 For the left feet, roll out some cream modelling paste between the narrow spacers and, using the template, cut out the two left feet with a cutting wheel. Stick in place on the board with sugar glue and then mark the hooves with a cutting wheel. For the right feet, roll the modelling paste to a thickness of 1.3cm (½in) and repeat (**M**).

Adding features

1 For the mouth, soften some of the golden-brown modelling paste. Do this by firstly kneading in some white vegetable fat to stop the paste becoming sticky and then partially dunking the paste into a small container of boiled water before kneading again (the paste should have the consistency of chewing gum). Place the softened paste with the 1.5 piping tube into the sugar shaper.

2 Take a fine paintbrush and some sugar glue and paint the outline of the giraffe's smile onto the face. Squeeze out a length of paste from the sugar shaper (if the paste doesn't come out easily the paste isn't soft enough) and place it over the painted glue. Cut to size on the cake using a craft knife. Paint on the corners of the mouth and add small lengths of brown paste, cut to size on the cake.

If you do not have a sugar shaper, pipe the outline with royal icing coloured to match the golden brown.

3 For the eyes and nostrils, colour a small amount of modelling paste dark brown and roll out thinly. Take the 1.5cm (⁹⁄₁₆in) and 6mm (¼in) oval cutters and cut two ovals of each size. Attach the larger ovals to the face for eyes and smaller ones for nostrils. Thinly roll out some cream modelling paste and cut two light spots with a 1.5 piping tube, and attach to the top of the eyes.

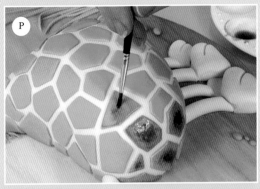

Decorating the board

1 For the leaves, roll out the green modelling paste between the narrow spacers and cut out a selection of paisley shapes or leaf shapes in four different sizes (**N**). Arrange the shapes in two layers at the top left-hand side of the board to represent the leaves of a tree.

2 For the grass, roll out the green modelling paste between the narrow spacers, then take the cutting wheel and run it backwards and forwards through the paste to create long, thin triangles (**O**). Cut across the base of the triangles and arrange on the lower right-hand corner of the board to represent grass. Use sugar glue to secure.

Stage Three

Painting the cake

1 Separately dilute some golden-brown and brown paste colours in clear spirit. Paint over a spot with some dilute golden-brown colour, then paint over the central area, using a stippling action, with a more intense golden-brown (**P**). Finally, paint the centre with the brown paste colour. Repeat for the other spots.

2 Paint the mane, tail and tufts on the horns with the golden-brown colour to highlight the texture, and then add a few touches of the brown colour to add interest. Using the brown colour, paint the hooves (**Q**).

3 Dilute some olive-green paste colour in clear spirit and paint over the leaves (**R**) and grass, being careful not to paint the board.

If you do accidentally paint the board, immediately remove the paint with a clean damp brush.

Finishing touches

Using a non-toxic glue stick, attach the ribbon around the sides of the board to complete the cake.

Mini-cakes

Bake oval-shaped bitesized cakes using the egg mini-cake pans (W) following the instructions on page 11. Cover the cakes with buttercream and then cream-coloured sugarpaste, and decorate as for the head using smaller cutters.

Animal Magic

Add 'Happy Birthday', a message or the recipient's name in a speech bubble to the right of the giraffe's neck.

❀

If you need to feed a large number of guests, bake a large slab cake and decorate it as the board has been decorated here and then place the giraffe cake on top.

❀

Take It Easy

He might be chilled and laid back, but this tortoise still likes to have fun! Carrying his beautifully sculpted and painted shell on his back, our slow-moving friend is absolutely realistic right down to his delicate claws and the scales on his skin. He has a captivating smile as he looks out onto the party table, and is sure to be admired by all the guests. Take your time with this project as there are some fine details, but the clear instructions help to make this advanced project achievable. The cake is accompanied by cup cakes topped with mini-tortoises.

Materials

- ✿ two 25.5 × 20cm (10 × 8in) rectangular Madeira cakes plus a 9cm (3½in) round (see pages 8–9)
- ✿ jam (optional)
- ✿ 1 quantity buttercream (plus extra if you wish to split and fill the cake)
- ✿ sugarpaste (rolled fondant): 1kg (2¼lb) golden brown, 1.6kg (3½lb) orange
- ✿ paste colours: golden brown (Spectral – Autumn Leaf), violet, mid orange (SK – Marigold), dark orange (SK – Nasturtium)

- ✿ icing (confectioners') sugar (optional)
- ✿ white vegetable fat (shortening)
- ✿ clear spirit, such as gin or vodka
- ✿ white dust colour (Sugarflair – Superwhite)
- ✿ sugar glue
- ✿ modelling paste: 15g (½oz) black
- ✿ confectioners' glaze

Use a food can for the 9cm (3½in) round cake.

Equipment

- ✿ greaseproof paper
- ✿ 38cm (15in) round cake drum (board)
- ✿ scriber or pencil
- ✿ palette knife
- ✿ cocktail sticks (toothpicks)
- ✿ waxed paper
- ✿ 5mm (³⁄₁₆in) spacers
- ✿ straightedge

- ✿ craft knife
- ✿ small scissors
- ✿ paintbrushes
- ✿ Dresden tool
- ✿ cutting wheel
- ✿ 14cm (5½in) dowel
- ✿ foam
- ✿ brown ribbon and non-toxic glue stick

Preparation

Preparing the cake for freezing

Level the two rectangular cakes. If you like, split and fill each cake with jam and buttercream. Spread buttercream over the top of one cake and stack the second on top. Make the outline template from greaseproof paper and place on top of the cake. With a knife, cut vertically through the cake around the template (**A**). Freeze the cake overnight.

Covering the board

1 Place the template on the board towards the back. Draw around the template, with either a scriber (**B**) or pencil. Take 50g (2oz) of the golden-brown sugarpaste and add shallow flattened balls to the outside of the shell outline to give the board depth and an uneven, natural appearance (**C**).

2 Add some golden-brown paste colour to the golden-brown sugarpaste and briefly knead to create a marbled effect in the paste.

3 Roll out the golden-brown sugarpaste using icing sugar or white vegetable fat to prevent sticking and use to cover the board. Using a palette knife, trim the edges flush with the sides of the board, taking care to keep the cut vertical. Place to one side to dry.

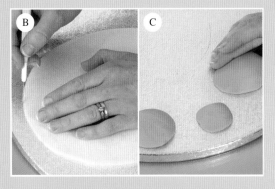

D

E

F

G

Stage One

Carving the body

1 Remove the cake from the freezer. Mark the position of the base of the shell and top of the frill section with cocktail sticks, as follows: for the base, place the cocktail sticks at a height of 6.5cm (2½in) at the front reducing to 3cm (1⅛in) by the middle of the sides. For the top of the frill section, place the cocktail sticks at a height of 9.5cm (3¾in) at the front, 7.5cm (3in) in the middle of the sides and 7cm (2¾in) at the back (see picture D).

2 Make a horizontal cut along the top line of cocktail sticks, cutting 2.5cm (1in) into the cake. Curve the top of the shell by cutting down from the top of the cake to the inside of the cut just made (**D**).

It is easier to remove the cake in small sections rather than trying to shape it all at once.

3 Cut from the edge of the top section of shell, the section just shaped, to the lower cocktail sticks using a slanting cut (**E**). Finally, cut a small wedge away from a lowest section of cake so that the shell tucks under the tortoise's body (**F**).

Carving the head

Level the small round cake for the head to a height of 5cm (2in). Remove from the sides of the cake two small sections to make the face more pointed as shown on the sketch on page 99. Reduce the height of the resulting nose to 3.5cm (1⅜in) then curve all the cut edges (see picture F).

Covering the cake

1 The cake is covered in sections. Place the shell cake on waxed paper and spread a thin layer of buttercream over to stick the sugarpaste. Take 500g (1lb 2oz) of orange sugarpaste and add this to the shell in sections, to help create the tortoise's distinctive shell shape, as follows. To create the frill sections, roll some sugarpaste into a ball and then a wide cone, flatten the shape in the palm of your hand and position onto the cake. Create small sections at the head end and larger ones towards the back. Smooth the paste to form the edge of the frill using your fingers. For the top sections, roll a ball and then flatten it in the palm of your hand. Position it on the cake (**G**) and blend the edges with your fingers.

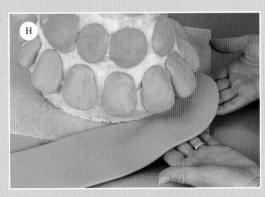

2 Roll out a strip of orange sugarpaste between the 5mm (³/₁₆in) spacers. Using a palette knife and a straightedge, cut the strip in half lengthways. Pick up one half of the paste and place it around one side of the lower section of the shell, so that the paste is positioned on one side between the head to tail, and the cut straight edge lies around the base of the cake (**H**). Place the second half in position and smooth the joins closed with the heat of your finger. The head and tail will cover the joins, so the paste does not need to be completely blended. Using a craft knife, cut away the excess paste from the top of this shell section (**I**).

3 To cover the frill section of the shell, roll out another strip of sugarpaste and cut in half. Place the straight edge of the strip around the inner line of the shell so that the excess paste overlaps the lower section already covered. As it is easier to fit and texture a small area at a time, cover, say, three or four frill sections and cut away the remainder of the strip. Next, using a small pair of scissors, cut away the excess paste from the edge of the frill (**J**) and soften the cut edge with a finger, smoothing the frill so that it follows the contours of the sugarpaste beneath.

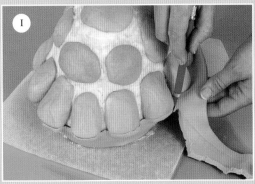

4 Add texture to the frill by using a straightedge. Hold the straightedge on its side, so that its flat surface rests on the sugarpaste (**K**) and press the edge sideways into the soft paste, that is, push it towards the centre of the section, to mark one of the side lines of the central rectangle.

Use a clear plastic ruler or set square so that the markings you've already made are not obscured.

5 Remove the straightedge and reposition to mark the top of the rectangle and then the other side; the lower edge of the frill forms the fourth side. Add further lines around the rectangle to create a closely textured surface (**L**). Repeat for the remaining covered frill sections.

6 Cover and texture the remaining frill sections. For the top of the shell, roll out the orange sugarpaste as before and cover, say, two or three sections at a time, cutting away any excess paste and blending any joins. Texture as for the frill but this time centralize the untextured area within each section. Leave to dry.

Stage Two

Painting the cake

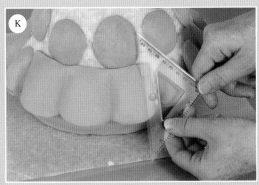

1 Carefully transfer the cake to the covered board. Slightly dilute the suggested paste colours in clear spirit in a paint palette. Mix a dark brown by combining the golden-brown and violet paste colours together; mix a light purple-brown by combining the white dust colour with violet and some of the dark brown colour you have just mixed. Using the dark brown colour, carefully paint over the lower section of shell, the area below the frill. To disguise any brushstrokes stipple the painted surface with a dry brush.

If you accidentally get paint onto your covered board use a clean damp brush to remove any traces.

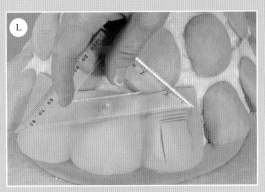

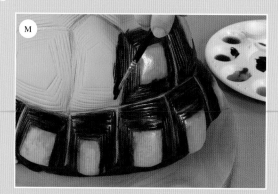

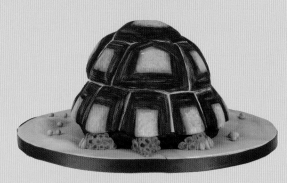

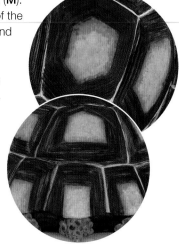

2 Using a reasonably fine paintbrush, paint lines of the very light purple-brown colour between each section of the shell to help emphasize the pattern markings. Next, using the mixed dark brown, paint over the textured lines of, say, three sections of shell (**M**). Change the brush and stipple over the centre of the sections with the mid orange (**N**) and then around the edges with the dark orange (**O**).

3 Stipple some dark brown colour around the edge of the centre so that the shape looks less regular.

4 Remove some lines of the paint from the painted brown area with a clean damp brush to lighten the colour, and then paint a few additional lines over the area using the golden-brown and violet paste colours to give a multicoloured effect.

Adding the legs and tail

1 For the right front leg, take 100g (3½oz) of orange sugarpaste and roll it into a thick, slightly tapered sausage. Bend the sausage into an L-shape and cut the larger end at an angle so that it will fit snugly against the lower shell section. Stick in place using sugar glue, leaving room for the neck.

2 For the left front leg, use 200g (7oz) of orange sugarpaste; roll a slightly longer tapered sausage, cut and position as for the right leg.

3 For the hind legs and tail, take 50g (2oz) of orange sugarpaste. Roll about a third into a small cone for the tail and stick in place. Make two flattened balls from the remaining sugarpaste and attach for legs.

Adding scales

Paint sugar glue over the legs and tail. Then roll small balls of sugarpaste and use to cover the legs and tail to represent the scales. Start at the tip of each leg and, when placing the balls, flatten each one slightly so that they abut one another (**P**).

Add a few larger elongated balls to the front legs to create a more interesting pattern.

Covering the head

1 Spread a thin layer of buttercream over the underside of the head to help stick the sugarpaste. Roll balls of sugarpaste as for the legs and attach to the underside of the head. Turn the head over and place on waxed paper.

2 Spread buttercream over the remaining cake. Then roll two 1cm (³⁄₈in) balls of black modelling paste and place on the head for eyes. Roll four small sausages of orange sugarpaste and place one under and over each eye to form eyelids. Cover the rest of the head cake with small balls as before. Indent two nostrils using a Dresden tool and a mouth with a cutting wheel. Place to one side.

Painting the legs and tail

Using diluted golden-brown paste colour, paint over the legs and tail and then stipple the centre of some scales with a stronger golden-brown colour. Next, add a touch of the dark brown mixed colour to the centre of most scales. Finally, remove the colour from the larger scales on the front legs with a damp brush and paint over with the dark orange.

Stage Three

Claws

Roll four small sausages of orange paste for each leg and attach to the ends of each leg to make claws.

Adding the neck

Roll 100g (3½oz) of orange sugarpaste into a short, fat sausage and position for a neck in between the front legs. Insert the dowel through the neck and into the cake, to help support the head.

Positioning the head

Carefully pick up the head and position on top of the neck and dowel, supporting it if necessary with foam while the sugarpaste sets.

Painting the neck and head

Using the dark brown paste colour, paint the neck as for the lower shell. Paint the head as for the legs, but adding an orange section to the front of his face and highlighting the nostrils and mouth with the dark brown paste colour.

Finishing touches

Glaze the eye with confectioners' glaze to add a shine. Roll a few small balls of brown sugarpaste and add to the board for stones. Using a non-toxic glue stick attach the ribbon around the sides of the board to complete the cake.

Animal Magic

Add the recipient's favourite football club's hat and scarf to the tortoise's head and neck.

❀

Colour the sugarpaste for the board green and add cut-out flowers.

❀

For a gardening enthusiast, make a brightly coloured hat for the tortoise decorated with cut-out flowers or cut out a rectangle of white modelling paste to make a seed packet and tuck it into a decorative hatband.

❀

Add 'Welcome to your new home' to the shell, as a house-warming gift.

❀

Personalize the cake by using letter cutters to add a name, age and/or 'Happy Birthday' to the board.

❀

Cup Cakes

Make the cup cakes following the instructions on page 10. Cover the top of each cake with a disc of slightly marbled golden-brown sugarpaste, as for the board. Make your own tortoise mould, following the instructions on page 13, or use a commercial mould to make a tortoise for each cake. Paint the tortoises as for the main cake and stick one to the top of each cup cake.

Pool Party

Swimming in a pale-turquoise pool, these elegant fish suggest the delicate creations of Japanese art. Here, two cakes are carefully carved and covered with sugarpaste, which is then decorated with cut-out shapes. The professional and sophisticated finish is achieved by painting over the bodies, fins and tails with paste colours, so allow plenty of time to work on these areas carefully. Such exotic fish must make the perfect party cake for an adult, but will be endearing to children as well, and they come complete with dainty fish or air-bubble cup cakes.

Materials

- ✿ 25.5cm (10in) round chocolate cake (see pages 8–9)
- ✿ sugarpaste (rolled fondant): 1kg (2¼lb) very pale blue (white with a hint of blue), 1kg (2¼lb) turquoise-blue
- ✿ icing (confectioners') sugar (optional)
- ✿ white vegetable fat (shortening)
- ✿ paste colours: turquoise, blue, green, lime-green, yellow
- ✿ clear spirit, such as gin or vodka
- ✿ 1 quantity buttercream
- ✿ sugar glue
- ✿ modelling paste: 225g (8oz) green, 25g (1oz) black
- ✿ confectioners' glaze
- ✿ piping gel

Equipment

- ✿ greaseproof paper
- ✿ glass-headed dressmaker's pins
- ✿ 40.5 × 35.5cm (16 × 14in) oval cake drum (board)
- ✿ palette knife
- ✿ paintbrushes including a flat-headed paintbrush and a stippling brush
- ✿ cocktail stick (toothpick)
- ✿ scriber (optional)
- ✿ 5mm (³/₁₆in) spacers
- ✿ smoother
- ✿ craft knife
- ✿ Dresden tool
- ✿ narrow spacers made from 1.5mm (¹/₁₆in) thick card
- ✿ cutting wheel
- ✿ Elegant Heart cutters (LC): 4cm (1½in), 2.3cm (¹⁵/₁₆in), 1.5cm (⁹/₁₆in)
- ✿ oval cutters: 2.3cm (¹⁵/₁₆in), 1.6cm (⁵/₈in), 1.2cm (¹⁵/₃₂in), 1cm (³/₈in)
- ✿ sugar shaper, with large round disc
- ✿ 2.5cm (1in) circle cutter
- ✿ no. 1 piping tube (tip)
- ✿ light blue ribbon and non-toxic glue stick

Preparation

Preparing the head cake for freezing
Enlarge the fish template so that it fits the cake board, and trace the body sections following the dotted lines onto greaseproof paper. Level the cake and place the templates on top, using dressmakers' pins to secure. Cut vertically through the cake along the outline of the template (**A**). Freeze the cake overnight.

Covering the board
Roll out the very pale-blue sugarpaste using icing sugar or white vegetable fat to prevent sticking. Place over the cake board. Trim the sugarpaste flush with the sides of the board, taking care to keep the cut vertical. Leave to dry.

Painting the board
Weakly dilute some of the turquoise paste colour in clear spirit to make a wash. Using a flat-headed paintbrush, apply the wash in roughly parallel strokes across the top of the board (**B**). Paint 7.5–10cm (3–4in) of the board then draw the tip of the brush repeatedly through the wet wash in an overlapping wave action to create a subtle pattern (**C**). Repeat the painting process until the board is completed, and leave to dry.

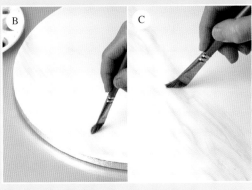

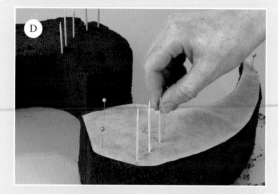

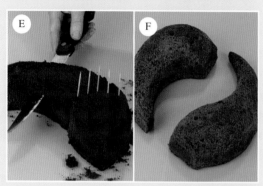

Stage One

Carving the cake

Remove the cake from the freezer. Place the body templates back on the cakes and insert cocktail sticks along the curved line on each head (**D**). Carefully lift off the templates. Take a large knife and make a sloping cut from the tip of the tail up to the cocktail sticks (**E**). For the head, place the knife at a height of 3.5cm (1³⁄₈in) against the mouth then make a curved sloping cut up to the cocktail sticks. Curve all the edges to give the fish a rounded appearance. Repeat for the second fish (**F**).

Covering the cake

1 Make another template, including the fins and tail and following the continuous line of the body. Place the template onto the prepared board and hold in place with pins. Take a scriber or pin and scribe around the outline of the fish (**G**) including the fins, so that the scribed lines are visible on the sugarpaste once the tracing is taken away.

Scribing tips

Designs are often scribed onto the board so that positioning the cake is easier and that additional decorations can be added precisely in position.

❀ Take care to place your template in the correct position on the covered board and that all of the design is inside the board perimeter.

❀ When you lay the template onto the board use dressmaker's pins in just a few places to secure it.

❀ A scriber is easier than a pin to use when tracing around the outline of a complicated shape, such as these fish.

❀ Make sure you press hard enough on the tracing so that the lines are visible on the board when the template is removed.

❀ When you remove the template, check that all the lines are clear and go over any that are particularly faint.

2 Place the top fish in position on the board. If necessary, add sugarpaste to the fish to adjust the shape to fit the scribed line, and then add a small amount to the tail to create a point (**H**). Spread a thin layer of buttercream over the cake. Remove any excess crumbs. Knead 600g (1lb 5oz) of the turquoise-blue sugarpaste until warm. Roll out the sugarpaste between the 5mm (³/₁₆in) spacers and place over the cake (**I**). Smooth to shape, using a smoother and the heat from your hand. Place the smoother against the outside of the body and run it along the side of the body, pressing down into the excess paste at the same time to create a cutting line in the sugarpaste (**J**). Repeat, as far as possible, for the inside edge. Cut away the excess paste (**K**).

3 Place the remaining cake in position, cover with buttercream and adjust the shape. Cover the cake with the remaining turquoise-blue sugarpaste; avoid touching the covered cake.

Stage Two

Mouth

1 Make a ball of the very pale-blue sugarpaste and roll over half of the ball, gradually exerting more pressure so that the thickness of the paste is gradually reduced. Cut out the template from the back of the mouth section of one of the fish as shown by the dotted line and place it so that the edge closest to the head is on the thickest area and the outer edge on the thinnest. Cut out the shape using a craft knife (**L**) and attach in place on the board so that the thicker edge joins up to the cake, with the thinner part on the outside. The rounded shape will form the inside of the mouth. Secure with sugar glue. Repeat for the second fish.

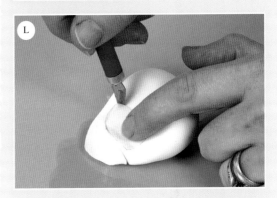

2 Roll out some turquoise-blue sugarpaste to a thickness of 1.25cm (½in). Place the lower jaw template onto the paste and cut out. Rub the lower edge of the curved cut with a finger to blend into a smooth curve (**M**). Paint a line of glue along the long straight cut. Place this cut below the back of the mouth and onto the lower section of the head of the lower fish, so that the small straight cut abuts the board and the blended curved edge creates the curve of the lower lip and the cut edge the lip. Blend the paste into the body using a finger and/or a Dresden tool; (the join will be partly covered later) (**N**). Turn the template over and repeat for the second fish.

When you are forming the mouth, check that you have correctly positioned the very pale-blue shape for the back of the mouth and the turquoise-blue lower jaw by looking at it from different angles and comparing it to the detail pictures shown.

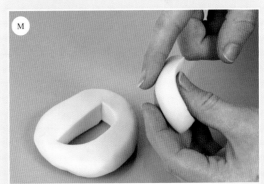

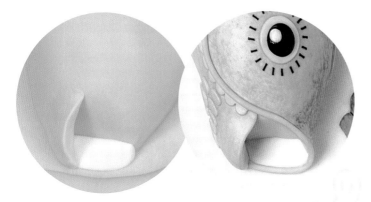

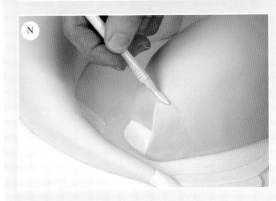

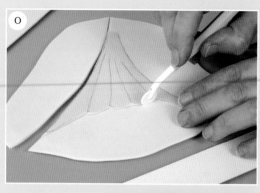

Fins

Cut out the fin templates. Knead the green modelling paste until warm, adding a little white vegetable fat and boiled water if necessary to make the paste elastic and workable, then roll out between the narrow spacers. Place one of the fin templates onto the paste and cut around it with a cutting wheel (**O**). Lightly roll the cutting wheel over the lines on the template. Remove the template and attach the paste fin in the appropriate place on the board using sugar glue to secure. Emphasize the marking on the fin with either the sharper end of the Dresden tool or a cutting wheel (**P**). Repeat for all the fins that lie on the board (the fins on the body are made later) (**Q**).

Painting the cake

1 Separately dilute some turquoise and blue paste colours in clear spirit. Use a stippling brush to stipple turquoise paste colour onto the upper fish (**R**), being careful not to paint the board and fins at the same time. Paint over the back of the fish with a fairly strong colour and the underside with a more dilute colour. If you wish to darken the colour, wait until the surface is dry and then paint over another coat. If you wish to lighten the colour wait until dry then use some damp kitchen paper to wipe away a little colour carefully, using a circular action.

2 Paint the lower fish, using the diluted blue paste over the back and diluted turquoise underneath. Leave to dry. Separately dilute some green and lime-green paste colour in clear spirit. Using sweeping strokes, apply the colour to the fins, painting the darker colour at the ends of the fins and a lighter one nearer the body (**S**). Blend the colours using a damp brush. (If you are not happy with the result, remove the colour with damp kitchen paper and start again.)

Stage Three

Gills

1 Using the templates and picture as a guide, scribe a gill line onto each fish and mark the position of the eyes. Roll out the green modelling paste between the narrow spacers and cut out about 12 hearts using the largest cutter. Paint a line of glue along the gill line of the upper fish and place a row of hearts over the line so that the widest sections of the hearts abut and the narrow ends point toward the position of the eye.

2 Using a cutting wheel, cut a line through the hearts where they abut, cutting more away from the shapes as they go towards the mouth. Remove all the points. Using the largest oval cutter repeat this sequence for the second fish.

3 To create the roof of the fishes' mouths, take some of the very pale-blue sugarpaste and make two small triangles of paste. Stick one above the back of the mouth on each fish to allow the top lip to protrude slightly. Blend the edges that lie adjacent to the bodies with a Dresden tool.

4 Soften some of the green modelling paste by kneading in some white vegetable fat and then partially dunking the paste into a small container of boiled water. Knead again (the paste should have the consistency of chewing gum). Place the softened paste with the large round disc into the sugar shaper.

5 Paint a line of glue on each fish around the gills, over the top of the mouth and down the back of the mouth. Squeeze out two lengths of paste from the sugar shaper and place onto the glued lines. Cut to size using a craft knife.

Eyes

1 Roll out the green modelling paste between the narrow spacers and cut out two 2.5cm (1in) circles. Attach one circle to each fish for an eye. Roll a 1.5cm (9/16in) wide ball of black modelling paste and cut in half, attach each half to the centre of a circle. Roll two small balls of very pale-blue sugarpaste and attach them to the pupils as light spots.

2 Soften the remaining black modelling paste (the paste should have the consistency of extremely soft chewing gum). Place the very soft paste with the piping tube into the sugar shaper.

3 Paint radial lines of glue around each eye with a fine paintbrush. Then squeeze out short lengths of thin, black paste from the sugar shaper. Place the lengths over the painted glue lines and cut to size with a craft knife.

Scales

1 Roll out the green modelling paste between the narrow spacers and cut out a selection of hearts and ovals. Attach hearts to the top fish and ovals to the lower fish, placing the larger shapes down the back of the fish and the smaller ones towards the tail.

2 Thinly roll out some of the turquoise-blue paste and cut out a number of small ovals. Attach these ovals to the area under the mouth on each fish to help disguise the join in the paste made earlier.

Side fins

Cut out the two remaining fins from green modelling paste, add the markings as before and attach in place. Support the upper fin in place with kitchen paper while the paste dries.

Painting

Separately dilute the turquoise, green and yellow paste colours with clear spirit and paint over the two remaining fins, the gills and the scales, using a stippling action for the scales.

Finishing touches

Using a non-toxic glue stick attach the ribbon around the sides of the board to complete the cake. Glaze the fishes' eyes by painting over the pupils with confectioners' glaze. Add a subtle shine to the board and fish by painting over the sugarpaste with a thin layer of white vegetable fat. (If using hard fat, melt it first). Add an extra layer of fat in the centre of the board to prevent the bubbles, added below, melting the painted pattern on the board. Warm some piping gel in a microwave or a heatproof bowl over a pan of simmering water until the gel is lump-free. Load a paintbrush and carefully place droplets of gel onto the board to represent bubbles.

Animal Magic

Change the colours of the fish to reds and oranges for goldfish or any colours you like for brightly coloured fish.

❀

If you need to feed a large number of guests bake a large slab cake and decorate it as the board has been decorated here and then place the fish on top.

❀

Personalize the cake by using letter cutters to add a name, age and/or 'Happy Birthday' to the space on the board.

❀

Cup Cakes

Make cup cakes following the instructions on page 10. Cover the top of each cup cake with a disc of very pale-blue sugarpaste. Paint over each disc as for the board. Once dry, cover with a layer of white vegetable fat. Add bubbles to some of the cakes and make cut-out fish for the remainder using the pastes and colours used for the main cake.

Purrfectly Exotic ♡

This elegant, white cat is lounging dreamily on luxurious and exotically decorated cushions, waiting to be invited to only the best kind of party. The background contains most of the decorative effects, which are simple to make using cut-out shapes. The feline form is carefully carved and covered with sugarpaste, and the stunning collar is decorated with sugar crystals. As the crystals can take a few weeks to grow, start making them well in advance. Cup cakes topped with the cushion pattern make a sophisticated accompaniment.

Materials

- ❀ 30 × 23cm (12 × 9in) Madeira cake (see pages 8–9)
- ❀ 25g (1oz) pastillage
- ❀ white vegetable fat (shortening)
- ❀ sugarpaste (rolled fondant): 1.1kg (2½lb) white, 600g (1lb 5oz) burgundy, 250g (8oz) red, 150g (5oz) orange, 200g (7oz) pink, 150g (5oz) claret
- ❀ gum tragacanth
- ❀ paste colours: burgundy, red, pink, orange
- ❀ clear spirit, such as gin or vodka
- ❀ 1 quantity buttercream
- ❀ sugar glue
- ❀ 4mm (⅛in) gold and silver dragées (sugar balls)
- ❀ sugar crystals for the collar (see page 18)

Start sugar crystals growing well in advance of making the cake.

- ❀ edible silver lustre dust
- ❀ confectioners' glaze
- ❀ 6mm (¼in) silver dragée
- ❀ mulberry sparkle dust

Equipment

- ❀ greaseproof paper
- ❀ sugar shaper with small round, large rope, fine mesh and medium round discs
- ❀ plastic sleeve
- ❀ craft knife
- ❀ 40.5 × 35.5cm (16 × 14in) oval cake drum (board)
- ❀ smoother
- ❀ 5mm (³⁄₁₆in) spacers
- ❀ palette knife
- ❀ paintbrushes
- ❀ stippling brush
- ❀ cocktail sticks (toothpicks)
- ❀ waxed paper
- ❀ Dresden tool
- ❀ narrow spacers made from 1.5mm (¹⁄₁₆in) thick card
- ❀ paisley cutters (LC)
- ❀ no. 18 piping tube (tip)
- ❀ Elegant Heart cutters (LC) 2.8cm (¹¹⁄₁₆in), 2cm (¾in)
- ❀ 1.5cm (⁹⁄₁₆in) 'cubby' heart cutter
- ❀ circle cutters: 3cm (1¹⁄₈in), 2cm (¾in), 7mm (⁹⁄₃₂in)
- ❀ burgundy ribbon and non-toxic glue stick

Preparation

Preparing the cake for freezing

Level the cake. Make body and head templates from greaseproof paper and place on top of the cake. Cut vertically through the cake around the outline of the templates (**A**). Remove the templates and freeze the cakes overnight.

Whiskers

Soften the pastillage. Do this by firstly kneading in some white vegetable fat to stop the paste becoming sticky and then partially dunking the paste into a small container of boiled water before kneading again (the paste should have the consistency of chewing gum). Place the softened paste with the small round disc into the sugar shaper. Place the whiskers template into a plastic sleeve then squeeze out lengths onto the template (**B**). Make extra whiskers in case of breakages. Pastillage, although strong, is also brittle. Cut to size with a craft knife. Leave to dry thoroughly; an airing cupboard is an ideal place.

Covering the board

1 Draw the cat's body onto the cake board by drawing around the template with a pencil. Add lines for the outlines of the cushions. Add approximately 100g (3½oz) of white sugarpaste to the two larger cushions and shape so that it is slightly raised in the middle and rounded, using a smoother (**C**).

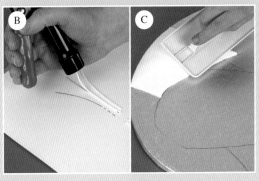

2 Roll out the burgundy sugarpaste between the 5mm (³/₁₆in) spacers and use to cover the top of the board. Take a smoother and, using a circular motion, smooth the paste to give a level surface. Using a palette knife, cut the paste away from the edges of the cushions, then trim the edges flush vertically with the sides of the board.

3 Roll out the red sugarpaste between the 5mm (³/₁₆in) spacers and use to cover the left-hand cushion, cut the cushion to size using a craft knife. Cover the cushion in the centre of the board with orange sugarpaste, and the right-hand cushion with pink sugarpaste. Cover the foreground with claret sugarpaste (see picture D). Leave to dry.

Making modelling paste

Take 50g (2oz) of the five colours of sugarpaste trimmings and knead in 1.5ml (¼ tsp) gum tragacanth to each to make modelling paste. Leave the paste to mature, ideally overnight.

Painting the board

Separately dilute some burgundy, red and pink paste colours in clear spirit. Use a flat-headed paintbrush to paint over the background burgundy sugarpaste with circular strokes, and then use scrunched-up kitchen paper to create a subtle pattern by going over the surface with a circular action (**D**). Take the stippling brush and stipple red paste colour onto the red cushion to intensify the colour, and pink to the pink cushion (**E**).

Stage One

Allow yourself time to get Stage One right.

Carving the cake

1 For the head, reduce the height of the nose to 5.5cm (2¼in) then curve all the top edges of the cake to give a rounded appearance to the head. Remove a small section of cake from around the base of the cake so that the head goes in slightly at the base (see picture H).

2 Remove the body cake from the freezer. Place the template back on the cake and insert cocktail sticks along the curved line of the hind leg (**F**). Carefully remove the template then reduce the height of the cake around the hind leg by 1.5cm (⁹/₁₆in) and reduce the neck to a height of 3cm (1⅛in).

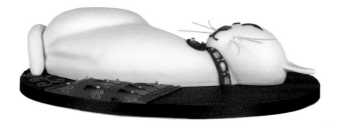

3 Curve all the cut edges of the body to round them (**G** and **H**). Remove a small wedge along the front of the cat to denote the front legs. Curve all the cut edges of the hind leg to give the leg a rounded appearance.

When curving the cake use a small knife and remove only a little cake at a time.

Covering the cake

Place the cakes on waxed paper. Spread a thin layer of buttercream over the body cake to stick the sugarpaste. Knead the white sugarpaste to warm it, and then roll it out between the 5mm (³/₁₆in) spacers. Pick up the paste and carefully place it over the cake. Ease in the fullness. Smooth the sugarpaste using a smoother and the palm of your hand to eliminate any irregularities in the surface. While you keep working the paste will remain pliable, so spend time perfecting the finish. Place the smoother against the outside of the body, and run it along the side of the body pressing down into the excess paste to create a cutting line in the sugarpaste. Cut away the excess paste from the base. Repeat for the head then leave to dry.

Making white modelling paste

Take 100g (3½oz) of the white sugarpaste trimmings and knead in 2.5ml (½ tsp) gum tragacanth. Leave the paste to mature, ideally overnight.

Stage Two

Decorating the cake and board

Transfer the cake to the prepared board, making sure it fits snugly between the cushions. Roll a narrow sausage of white sugarpaste and place it around the neck of the cat where the two cakes join. Blend the paste into the cat with the flatter end of the Dresden tool.

When placing the head and body on the board, position the head to leave enough space for the ears.

Orange cushion

1 Roll out the orange and burgundy modelling pastes using the narrow spacers and, using the two smallest paisley cutters, cut a selection of shapes (**I**). Attach the larger ones randomly to the orange cushion and then add smaller ones in the contrasting colour on top of some of the shapes.

2 Soften some of the burgundy modelling paste by kneading in some white vegetable fat and then partially dunking the paste into a small container of boiled water before kneading again (the paste should have the consistency of chewing gum). Place the paste with the small round disc into the sugar shaper. Paint sugar glue around the orange paisley shapes, adding a curl to the end of each. Squeeze out lengths of paste and place over the glue, cutting to size with a craft knife. Repeat with orange modelling paste around the burgundy shapes.

3 Roll out the red and burgundy modelling pastes between the narrow spacers, and cut out small circles using the no. 18 piping tube. Attach the burgundy circles to the spaces on the cushion and the red ones to the paisley shapes. Add gold dragées to the centre of some of the small circles and paisley shapes.

4 Use the large rope disc in the sugar shaper to squeeze out two lengths. Twist each length to form a rope and, using sugar glue, attach to the top and side edges of the cushion. Use the fine mesh disc to squeeze out lengths to form the tassels. Attach to the corners of the cushion (**J**).

Pink cushion

1 Roll out the pink and burgundy modelling pastes between the narrow spacers, then cut out pink hearts using the 2.8cm (11/16in) Elegant Heart cutter. Cut out some burgundy hearts using the 2cm (¾in) Elegant Heart cutter. Attach the pink ones in lines to the pink cushion and then add smaller burgundy ones to the spaces in-between. Attach a silver dragée to the tip of each small heart (see picture K).

2 To add trim to the cushion, soften some pink modelling paste and place in the sugar shaper with the medium round disc. Paint lines of glue along the edges of the cushion. Squeeze out two lengths of paste from the sugar shaper and place on the glue. Use the sharper end of a Dresden tool to indent the paste repeatedly to create a pattern (**K**).

Foreground

Using a fine paintbrush, paint sugar glue swirls onto the claret sugarpaste of the foreground. Soften some of the orange modelling paste. Place with the small round disc into the sugar shaper. Squeeze out lengths of paste and place over the glue, cutting to size with a craft knife.

Flowers

Roll out some of the modelling pastes between the narrow spacers and cut out a selection of petals using cutters that you have available. Arrange the shapes onto the board to create abstract flowers in the space above the red cushion (see main picture). Add centres using paste and dragées.

Mouth

Thinly roll out some pink modelling paste and cut out a 'cubby' heart. Stick to the head for a nose. Using a fine paintbrush, paint the mouth using sugar glue. Soften some of the burgundy modelling paste. Place with the small round disc into the sugar shaper. Squeeze out two lengths of paste and place over the glue, cutting to size with a craft knife (**L**).

Eyes

Using a fine paintbrush, paint the eyes onto the cake using sugar glue. Squeeze out some lengths of paste from the sugar shaper and place over the glue, cutting to size with a craft knife (**M**).

Painting the cushions and flowers (optional)

Dilute some of the paste colours in clear spirit and paint over the cushion (**N**), the foreground, flower decoration, and the mouth, nose and eyes, to enhance the look, if you like.

Collar

1 Select a number of similar-shaped crystals. Mix some silver lustre dust with confectioners' glaze and paint onto the back of the crystals (**O**).

2 Roll out some of the red sugarpaste between the 5mm ($^3/_{16}$in) spacers and cut a 1.5cm ($^9/_{16}$in) wide strip. Cut the strip in half, and then cut across each half of the strip at an angle so that the ends will fit snugly under the cat's chin. Attach the strips in place using sugar glue.

3 Press the prepared crystals into the soft sugarpaste at intervals along the collar then add silver dragées. Cut out three circles, using the circle cutters, from thinly rolled modelling paste and attach under the cat's chin. Top with a 6mm (¼in) silver dragée.

Tail

Roll a thick sausage of white sugarpaste, and wrap around the base of the cat for a tail, cut to size and smooth into place (**P**).

Ears

Roll out the white modelling paste between the 5mm (³⁄₁₆in) spacers. Place the ear template over the paste and cut around it with a craft knife. Turn the template over and cut a second ear (**Q**). Soften the cut edges by rubbing a finger along the edges of the cuts. Using a paintbrush, paint lines of sugar glue on either side of the head then pick up the ears and place onto the glue. Support in place if necessary with kitchen paper.

Paint the glue line on the head in a slight curve so that when you place the ears on top they will be gently curved rather than flat.

Whiskers

Insert a cocktail stick into the sugarpaste where each whisker is to go. Place a little sugar glue on the end of each pastillage whisker and insert into the prepared holes (**R**).

Finishing touches

Dust some mulberry sparkle dust over the foreground and the claret flower and hearts. Using a non-toxic glue stick, attach the ribbon around the sides of the board.

Animal Magic

Change the type, colour and style of the board decoration.

❀

Personalize the cat by changing its colour or adding markings.

❀

Personalize the cake by using letter cutters to add a name, age and/or 'Happy Birthday' to the board.

❀

Cup Cakes

Make cup cakes following the instructions on page 100. Cover the cup cakes with discs of sugarpaste made from the sugarpaste trimmings. Paint and decorate each with paisley shapes and hearts as for the main cake.

Top Dog

This little pup has just popped in because he heard there was a party going on and just couldn't possibly miss it. He has large, appealing eyes and a bright red tongue, and looks ready to jump up and play. Form his body and head with care using the carving instructions, as getting the correct main shape is extremely important for a successful finish. His sugarpaste covering and markings, however, are fairly straightforward. This pup will be top dog with children and dog lovers everywhere and comes complete with bone-shaped, decorated cookies.

Materials

❀ 30 × 18cm (12 × 7in) rectangular Madeira (see pages 8–9)

❀ sugarpaste (rolled fondant): 2kg (4½lb) blue divided into four 500g (1lb 2oz) pieces of different blues, 1.35kg (3lb) ivory, 25g (1oz) black

❀ icing (confectioners') sugar (optional)

❀ white vegetable fat (shortening)

❀ 1 quantity buttercream

❀ sugar glue

❀ gum tragacanth

❀ modelling paste: 50g (2oz) brown, 50g (2oz) red, 15g (½oz) white, 50g (2oz) black

❀ piping gel

Equipment

❀ greaseproof paper
❀ glass-headed dressmakers' pins
❀ 35.5cm (14in) square cake drum (board)
❀ 4mm (⅛in) spacers
❀ textured rolling pin or embosser (optional)
❀ straightedge
❀ palette knife
❀ smoother
❀ cocktail sticks (toothpicks)
❀ scriber (optional)
❀ 5mm (³/₁₆in) spacers
❀ Dresden tool
❀ craft knife
❀ narrow spacers made from 1.5mm (¹/₁₆in) thick card
❀ cutting wheel
❀ pan scourer (new)
❀ 4.5 × 2.5cm (1¾ × 1in) narrow oval cutter (FMM geometric set)
❀ no. 17 piping tube (tip) (optional)
❀ 1.3cm (½in) petal/teardrop cutter
❀ paintbrush
❀ blue ribbon and non-toxic glue stick

Preparation

Preparing the cake for freezing

Level the cake. Make a template from greaseproof paper, excluding the foreleg and tail, and place on top of the cake using pins. Cut vertically through the cake around the edges of the template (**A**). Remove the template and freeze the cake overnight.

Covering the board

1 Score two pencil lines diagonally across the cake board between the corners to divide it into four triangles. Roll out the darkest blue sugarpaste into a 35.5cm (14in) long sausage. Using a rolling pin, roll across the sausage diagonally from both ends to encourage the paste into a triangle shape (using icing sugar or white vegetable fat to prevent sticking). Place the 4mm (⅛in) spacers either side of the paste and continue rolling until the paste is the same thickness as the spacers. Place the paste over one triangle on the board.

2 Texture the paste, if you wish, with a textured rolling pin or embosser. Cut the paste to shape using a straightedge and a palette knife. Trim the outer edge flush vertically with the edge of the board. Roll out the second darkest colour. Cut one edge of the triangle straight; place this straight edge so that it abuts the right side of the textured triangle. Take a smoother and smooth the paste. Cut to shape (**B**). Add the other two colours so that they get lighter as they go anticlockwise around the board. Cut the last triangle so that it abuts the first. Leave to dry.

Save time by covering the board in one colour and indenting the diagonal lines over the sugarpaste with a cutting wheel and straightedge.

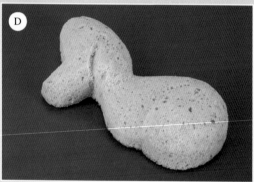

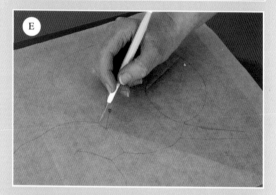

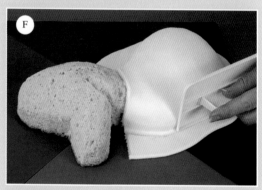

Stage One

Carving the cake

1 Remove the cake from the freezer. Return the template to the cake and insert cocktail sticks along the curved line of the hind leg and along the line of the neck. Carefully remove the template and reduce the height of the cake between the cocktail sticks, by 2.5cm (1in) below the neck and 1.3cm (½in) above the hind leg (**C**). Remove the cocktail sticks. Curve the straight edge along the back of the dog and then reduce the height of the chest area, curving the cake down towards the base.

Allow yourself time to get this right.

2 Curve all the cut edges of the hind leg to give a rounded appearance. Look at the profile picture to see the way the form is created for the finished cake to help you to carve the cake.

When curving the cake, use a small knife and remove only a little cake at a time.

3 To carve the head, place a cocktail stick centrally on the area that will be under the ear and in line with the nose, as this will stay at full height and the rest of the cake will be reduced. Reduce the height of the snout at its tip to 3cm (1⅛in) and its base, where it meets the face, to 6cm (2⅜in), by holding your knife horizontally and making a sloping cut. Then make a curved cut from the base of the nose towards the cocktail stick.

4 Reduce the height of the top of the head to 5cm (2in), by holding the knife horizontally and making a sloping cut from the tip of the head up to the cocktail stick. Curve all the cut edges to create a rounded appearance. With the point of a small knife, cut away a thin wedge of cake to create the side of the mouth (**D**).

Positioning the cake

Make another template of the dog, including the foreleg and tail. Secure it to the board with pins so that the dog is sitting in the textured darkest blue triangle, and the join at the back of the neck and head is just over the centre of the board where the four blue triangles meet. Scribe around the outline with a scriber or pin, then scribe a line down the centre of the dog's tail and the centre of the foreleg to mark their positions on the board (**E**). Carefully place the cake onto the board within the scribed outline.

Covering the cake

To ensure a neat and professional finish, the cake is covered in stages.

The body

1 Spread a thin layer of buttercream over the body and hind leg of the cake to stick the sugarpaste. Roll out 500g (1lb 2oz) of ivory sugarpaste between the 5mm (³⁄₁₆in) spacers and place it over the body of the dog. Smooth the cake by firstly using a smoother to iron out any irregulars in the surface of the icing and then the base of your hand to smooth and polish all the curves. Then take the smoother and, while pressing down, run the flat edge around the base of the cake to create a cutting line (**F**). Cut away the excess paste.

2 Run the back of the larger end of a Dresden tool along the join between the hind leg and body (**G**). Make two indentations from the neck across the top of the back.

The foreleg

Roll 50g (2oz) of ivory sugarpaste into a tapered sausage. Place onto the template and cut the larger end with a palette knife to fit the template (**H**). Place some sugar glue on the cut and position the leg over the scribed leg line. Using a smoother or straightedge, ensure that the leg is in line with the base of the body (**I**). Blend the paste at the top of the leg into the body with the flat side of a Dresden tool (**J**) and then a finger. Roll two 1.5cm (⁹⁄₁₆in) balls of sugarpaste and place on the end of the foot for toes.

Cover the join with a patch later if the join will not disappear completely.

Hind legs

Roll two sausages of paste, one larger than the other. Flatten the thinner one and cut across both at an angle so that they fit onto the base of the body. Attach the flattened sausage first, followed by the other. Blend the joins between the paste and the cake with the heat of a finger and then use a smoother to flatten into shape. Add balls of paste for toes.

Creating the lower jaw

Roll a small sausage of black sugarpaste and press it into the carved mouth indentation. Shape the remaining black sugarpaste to form the lower jaw, as shown (**K**).

Head

Spread a thin layer of buttercream over the head. Roll out the remaining ivory sugarpaste and cover all of the head but excluding the lower jaw. Gently ease in the paste so that it fits snugly, then run the flat edge of a smoother over the excess paste at the base of the cake. Cut this part away with a palette knife, being careful not to damage the covered board. Cut away the excess paste at the neck and blend the join, then take a craft knife and carefully cut away the paste to reveal the black sugarpaste at the sides of the mouth. Using a Dresden tool indent two lines over the bridge of the nose and the curve at the end of the mouth.

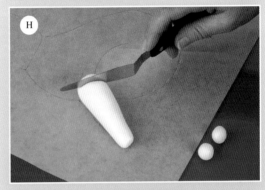

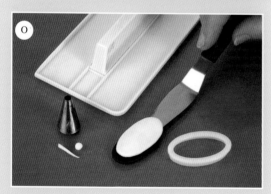

Covering the lower jaw

Roll out the ivory sugarpaste and, using a straightedge and palette knife, cut one edge straight. Place the cut edge of the paste along the top of the lower jaw to create the lower lip, ease the paste into shape and cut away the excess. Blend the join closed with the heat of a finger.

Making modelling paste

Take 100g (3½oz) of the ivory sugarpaste trimmings and knead in 2.5ml (½ tsp) gum tragacanth to make modelling paste. Leave the modelling paste to mature, ideally overnight.

Stage Two

If you are short of time this can be done the same time as Stage One.

Tail

Roll a slightly tapered sausage of ivory sugarpaste to fit the template. Cut across the larger end at an angle and position on top of the scribed line on the board. Blend the join between the tail and body with the heat of a finger.

Achieve a smooth tail by using a smoother to help you roll.

Patches

Roll out the brown modelling paste between the narrow spacers and cut patches in various sizes and shapes freehand with a cutting wheel (**L**). Attach to the body using sugar glue.

Tongue and nose

Make a tongue template and then roll out the red modelling paste between the 5mm (³⁄₁₆in) spacers. Place the template over the tongue and cut around it with a cutting wheel. Mark a central line with a Dresden tool (**M**), and then press a pan scourer over the paste for texture (**N**). Attach the back of the tongue to the back of the mouth and arrange. Roll some of the black modelling paste into a 3cm (1¹⁄₈in) ball. Attach in place for a nose.

Eyes

Roll out some of the white and black modelling paste between the narrow spacers. Cut out two white and four black ovals. Take two of the black ovals and press down on them with a smoother to enlarge them slightly. Place the white ovals centrally on top of the enlarged black ovals (**O**) and then place the remaining black ovals partially on top of the white, so that they overlap the edges of the white. Cut away the excess with a cutting wheel. Cut one eye in half and attach in place using sugar glue. Cut a small dot using the piping tube, and a small triangle with a craft knife, and add to the top of each pupil for a light spot (**P**).

Eyebrow

Using a fine paintbrush, paint sugar glue lines for the eyebrows. Roll a 9cm (3½in) long sausage of ivory modelling paste, cut it in half and place one half over the glue line over the whole eye. Cut the other section in half and place over the glue line above the half-eye.

If your modelling paste is dry and crumbly, add some white vegetable fat and boiled water, and knead well.

Ears

Roll out the ivory modelling paste between the narrow spacers and cut out an ear using the ear template. Paint a line of glue on the top side of the head, turn over the top of the ear and attach in position (**Q**). For the second ear, roll a short sausage, flatten and attach to the top of the head.

Finishing touches

Roll four short sausages of blue sugarpaste and place two either side of the tail to suggest movement. Cut out three teardrops from blue sugarpaste using the petal/teardrop cutter and attach to the board below the tongue. Then warm some piping gel either in a microwave or in a heatproof bowl over a pan of simmering water until the gel is lump-free. Load a paintbrush and add enough gel to the cut shapes to cover completely (**R**). Using a non-toxic glue stick, attach the ribbon around the sides of the board to complete the cake.

Cookies

Using bone cookie cutters (W), make the cookies as described on page 12. Once cool, ice with cream and brown royal icing as described on page 12. Use a cocktail stick (toothpick) to drag one colour of icing into the next to make interesting patterns or for a feathered look.

Animal Magic

Change the colour and markings, perhaps to make him look like a favourite dog.

❀

Make a brightly coloured dog coat with a message or a name, or add crazy cut-out decorations to make a wacky dog.

❀

Add a collar, perhaps with diamanté effect, as used for Purrfectly Exotic.

❀

Personalize the cake by using letter cutters to add a name, age and/or 'Happy Birthday' to the spaces on the board around the dog.

❀

Flower Power

With a large flower by her ear and holding another in her trunk, this delightful elephant is ready to take part in any festivity. She is standing against a pink background decorated with tiny flowers and is sure to win the heart of any little girl or small child. The elephant's curvaceous form is carved in stages to give a perfect base for the sugarpaste covering, which is applied in pieces – each section smoothed to a fine finish. Dainty, pink mini-cakes and bitesized cakes, decorated with flowers and a mini-elephant, continue the theme.

Materials

- ✿ sugarpaste (rolled fondant): 1kg (2¼lb) pink, 800g (1¾lb) grey with a touch of brown
- ✿ icing (confectioners') sugar (optional)
- ✿ white vegetable fat (shortening)
- ✿ 25.5cm (10in) round Madeira cake (see pages 8–9)
- ✿ jam (optional)
- ✿ 1 quantity buttercream, plus extra if you wish to split and fill the cake.
- ✿ gum tragacanth
- ✿ modelling paste: 50g (2oz) white, 15g (½oz) black, 10g (¼oz) green
- ✿ sugar glue
- ✿ edible pink dust

Equipment

- ✿ 33cm (13in) heart-shaped cake drum (board)
- ✿ smoother
- ✿ palette knife
- ✿ greaseproof paper
- ✿ glass-headed dressmakers' pins
- ✿ cocktail sticks (toothpicks)
- ✿ waxed paper
- ✿ 5mm (³⁄₁₆in) spacers
- ✿ straightedge
- ✿ Dresden tool
- ✿ narrow spacers made from 1.5mm (¹⁄₁₆in) thick card
- ✿ 1.6cm (⁵⁄₈in) circle cutter (wide end of piping tube)
- ✿ craft knife
- ✿ cutting wheel
- ✿ small piece of clear flexible plastic such as cut from a plastic bottle or milk carton
- ✿ small scissors
- ✿ oval cutter – 2.3cm (¹⁵⁄₁₆in)
- ✿ no. 16 piping tube (tip) (optional)
- ✿ soft paintbrush
- ✿ blossom cutters: 5cm (2in) (FMM Large Blossom set), 2.5cm (1in) (FMM Large Blossom set), 1.3cm (½in) (PME plunger set)
- ✿ pale-pink ribbon and non-toxic glue stick

Preparation

Covering the board

Roll out the pink sugarpaste using icing sugar or white vegetable fat to prevent sticking, and use to cover the board. Take a smoother and, using a circular motion, smooth the paste to give a level surface. Using a palette knife, trim the edges flush with the sides of the board, taking care to keep the cut vertical. Place to one side to dry.

Preparing the cake for freezing

1 Level the cake, and split and fill with layers of jam and buttercream as desired. Make a template from greaseproof paper and place on top of the cake. Secure with glass-headed dressmakers' pins. With a knife, cut vertically through the cake around the edges of the template (**A**).

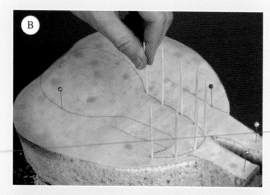

2 Insert cocktail sticks around the outline of the head and trunk (**B**) and then carefully lift off the template. Take a large knife and reduce the height of the elephant's legs and body to 5cm (2in) by cutting horizontally up to the cocktail sticks (**C**). Remove the cocktail sticks and freeze the cake overnight.

Stage One

Carving the cake

Remove the cake from the freezer. Mark the position of the legs with cocktail sticks and then curve all the outside edges of the body (**D**). Next, place the knife on the soles of the feet, 3cm (1⅛in) above the base of the cake and carefully make a diagonal cut up to the top of the legs (**E**). Cut away cake from the sides of the leg then curve all the edges of the legs to give a rounded appearance. Reduce the height of the tip of the trunk and then curve all edges of the head and trunk.

Covering the cake

The cake is covered in sections. Place the cake on waxed paper and spread a thin layer of buttercream over to stick the sugarpaste (**F**). Create a rounded appearance to the trunk and head. Do this by firstly taking 75g (3oz) grey sugarpaste and rolling it into a large ball, flattening the ball onto the face of the elephant and using a smoother to help blend the edges into the cake. For the trunk, roll 20g (¾oz) of sugarpaste into a tapered sausage and place over the cake, blend into the cake with a smoother, then adjust the shape as necessary (**G**).

Front left leg

Knead the grey sugarpaste until warm, and roll out about 100g (3½oz) between the 5mm (³⁄₁₆in) spacers. Using a straightedge and a palette knife, cut two edges straight to form a right angle. Pick up the paste and place one straight edge on the inside of the leg so that it touches the waxed paper, and the other up against the trunk. Smooth the paste around the sides of the leg and ease in the fullness around the foot. Take a smoother, place it against the base of the foot and press down to create a cutting line, repeat for the outside of the leg (**H**), then cut away the excess paste using a palette knife.

Front right leg

Roll out about 100g (3½oz) sugarpaste between the 5mm (³⁄₁₆in) spacers. Using a palette knife and a straightedge cut one edge straight, and then remove a curve from the top of this edge, so that the paste will fit around the elephant's trunk. Pick up the paste and place over the left-hand leg so that the straightedge is on the inside of the leg and the curve fits around the trunk (**I**). Smooth and ease into shape as before, then cut away the excess from the body and around the base.

The knees

Take a Dresden tool and, using the narrower end, make three indentations on each leg to represent the knees (**J**).

Right side of the body

Roll out about half of the remaining grey sugarpaste between the 5mm (³⁄₁₆in) spacers. Using a straightedge and a palette knife cut one edge straight. Pick up the paste and place the cut edge against the left-hand side of the head and left leg. Ease the paste into shape. Run the flat edge of a smoother over the excess paste at the base of the cake and cleanly cut this away with a palette knife (**K**). Then blend the paste between the body and the leg with the back of the larger end of the Dresden tool. Smooth the edges with a finger to round. Vertically cut away the sugarpaste at the top of the head.

Head and left side of the body

1 Roll out the remaining sugarpaste and cut one edge straight. Pick up the paste and place over the left-hand side of the body and head so that the straight edge abuts the paste on the right side of the body. Ease the paste over the head, trunk and body, then run the flat edge of a smoother over the excess sugarpaste at the base of the cake and cleanly cut this away with a palette knife.

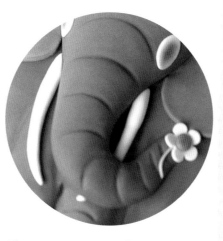

2 Cut away the excess paste at the top of the right side of the head, then blend the join with the larger end of a Dresden tool and a finger as before. Repeat for the area where the body meets the left leg. Indent around the left side of the head and around the trunk with a Dresden tool.

3 Next, define the top of the left leg with the Dresden tool. Finally, using the Dresden tool, mark curved lines onto the trunk and blend the upper edge of each indent with a finger to flatten and smooth. Set aside to dry.

Making modelling paste

Take 100g (3½oz) of the grey sugarpaste trimmings and knead in 2.5ml (½ tsp) gum tragacanth to make modelling paste. Leave the paste to mature, ideally overnight.

A Dresden tool is one of the most useful tools for marking and indenting sugarpaste and for blending joins before using the heat of your finger to make them disappear.

If you are pushed for time use CMC instead of gum tragacanth, as it reacts much quicker.

Stage Two

Decorating the cake

Carefully transfer the cake to the covered board, supporting the legs as you do so.

Toenails

Mix a small amount of grey and white modelling pastes together to make a slightly lighter grey. Roll out this paste between the narrow spacers and cut out six 1.6cm (⁵⁄₈in) circles. Using sugar glue, attach three to each foot so that they fractionally overlap the edge of the cake. Then take a craft knife and cut the circles flush with the soles of the feet. Neaten the appearance of the soles of the feet by running a cutting wheel over the join between the nails and sole (see right).

The wide end of the piping tube makes an excellent circle cutter.

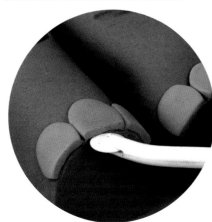

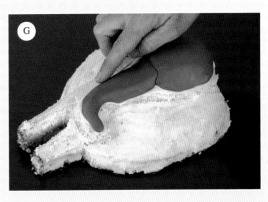

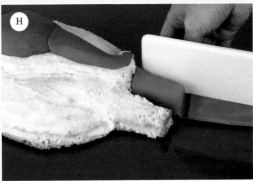

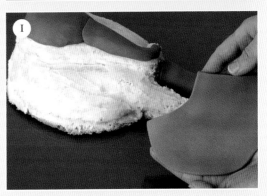

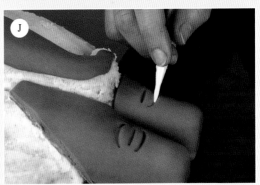

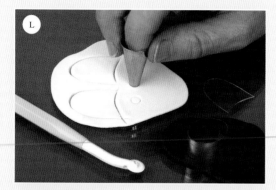

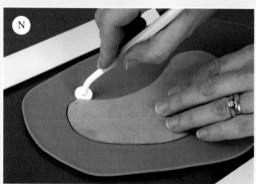

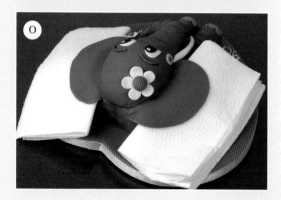

Eyes

1 Place some clear plastic over the eye template and trace it onto the plastic using a pencil (the pencil will indent the surface to give a cutting line). Cut around the traced lines with a small pair of scissors then place the template to one side. Individually roll out some of the white and black modelling pastes. Place the eye template onto the white paste and cut around it with a cutting wheel. Turn the template over and cut a second eye. Take the oval cutter and cut two ovals from the black modelling paste.

2 Place the ovals – the pupils – onto one side of the whites of the eyes then trim off the excess paste with a cutting wheel. Attach in place on the cake using sugar glue, then add a light spot to each eye by either adding small balls of white paste or circles cut with a no. 16 tube from thinly rolled paste (**L**).

Tusks

Roll some of the white modelling paste into a tapered sausage, approximately 9cm (3½in) long. Cut across the fatter end of the sausage at approximately 45 degrees, and attach to the top of the left side of the trunk. Carefully curve the tip of the tusk inwards. Repeat, but this time remove a section of sausage so that the tusk fits neatly either side of the curved end of the trunk.

You might find a smoother helpful when rolling the sausage.

Tail

Take some of the grey modelling paste and roll into a 2.5cm (1in) long tapered sausage, cut the fatter end at an angle and attach in position. Roll a thin sausage and cut into four 2cm (¾in) lengths. Roll the ends of each length to a point and attach to the end of the tail with sugar glue.

Eyebrows

Roll a thin sausage of grey modelling paste and cut into two 4cm (1½in) lengths. Roll the ends of each length to soften the cut edges and attach in position above the eyes with sugar glue.

Cheeks

Add a small amount of the pink sugarpaste to the remaining white modelling paste to create a pale-pink paste. Thinly roll out a small amount and cut two 2.3cm (¹⁵⁄₁₆in) ovals and attach in position. Take the pink dust and a soft brush, and dust the centre of each cheek to darken.

Flowers

1 Very thinly roll out the green modelling paste and cut into seven lengths, and slightly curve each to create flower stems. Place one at the top of the trunk and three either side of the feet. Using a straightedge and a craft knife, cut the lower end of the stems so that they are in line with the feet.

Create uniform stems by using a sugar shaper, if you have one, fitted with the small round disc.

2 Roll out the remaining pink modelling paste and cut one large flower, one medium flower and six small flowers using blossom cutters (**M**). Attach in position on the elephant and board as shown in the main picture. Add the flower centres by rolling pink sugarpaste balls of an appropriate size and placing them in the centre of each flower.

Ears

Roll out half the grey modelling paste between the narrow spacers. Place the ear template over the paste and cut around it with a cutting wheel (**N**). Paint a line of glue around one side of the head and attach the ear in position. Take some folded kitchen paper and place it under the ear to support the paste while it dries (**O**). Repeat for the second ear, remembering to turn the template over.

Finishing touches

Using a non-toxic glue stick attach the ribbon around the sides of the board to complete the cake.

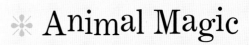

Animal Magic

Change the background colour and the colours of the flowers.

❀

Make a green background and add tall jungle grasses and bold flowers, and perhaps a brightly coloured cut-out bird, such as a parrot.

❀

Personalize the cake by using letter cutters to add a name, age and/or 'Happy Birthday' to the space on either side of the elephant.

❀

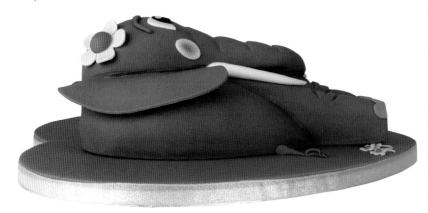

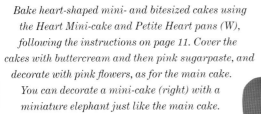

Mini-cakes

*Bake heart-shaped mini- and bitesized cakes using the Heart Mini-cake and Petite Heart pans (**W**), following the instructions on page 11. Cover the cakes with buttercream and then pink sugarpaste, and decorate with pink flowers, as for the main cake. You can decorate a mini-cake (right) with a miniature elephant just like the main cake.*

Farmyard Feast

Five party-going pigs, with bright hats, are sitting down on cake hay bales to a fantastic feast of sandwiches, carrots, chocolate mini-rolls, jam tarts and crisps, washed down with a drink of fizzy pop. Balloons and streamers help the party to go off with a bang. Although there's a lot of work in this busy party scene, each stage is quite straightforward and the pigs are simple to create and can be posed to hold the food. It's sure to be a hit with young children, who will also adore the cup cakes.

Materials

- sugarpaste (rolled fondant): 1kg (2¼lb) brown, 1kg (2¼lb) cream
- white vegetable fat (shortening)
- 15 × 20cm (6 × 8in) rectangular chocolate cake (see pages 8–9)
- 1 quantity buttercream
- paste colour: golden brown (Spectral – Autumn Leaf), plus assorted colours for sandwich fillings
- clear spirit, such as gin or vodka
- modelling paste: 450g (1lb) for pigs (coloured as you like), 15g (½oz) black, 25g (1oz) blue, 25g (1oz) green, 25g (1oz) red, 15g (½oz) white, 25g (1oz) orange
- dried spaghetti
- sugar glue
- piping gel
- confectioners' glaze

Equipment

- 5mm (³/₁₆in) spacers
- 25.5 × 30cm (10 × 12in) rectangular cake drum
- smoother
- palette knife
- pan scourer (new)
- waxed paper
- trellis embosser (PC)
- straightedge
- Dresden tool
- stiff kitchen brush (new)
- piping tubes (tips): nos 4, 16, 18
- paintbrushes
- cocktail sticks (toothpicks)
- small scissors
- narrow spacers made from 1.5mm (¹/₁₆in) thick card
- circle cutters: 3.25cm (1¼in) (FMM Geometric set), 2.4cm (³¹/₃₂in) (FMM Geometric set), 1.6cm (⁵/₈in) (wide end of piping tube), 1.3cm (½in)
- foam
- ball tool
- 1cm (³/₈in) square cutter
- craft knife
- sugar shaper with small mesh and small ribbon discs
- barbecue skewers
- cutting wheel
- red ribbon and non-toxic glue stick

Preparation

Covering the board

Roll out the brown sugarpaste between the 5mm (³/₁₆in) spacers. Lift up the paste, using a rolling pin for support, and place it over the board. Take a smoother and, using a circular motion, smooth the paste to give a level surface. Using a palette knife, trim the edges flush with the sides of the board. Take a pan scourer and firmly press it into the soft paste to add texture (**A**). Re-cut the edges, taking care to keep the cut vertical. Place to one side to dry.

Stage One

Carving the cake

1 Straighten the sides of the cake, if necessary. Using a long-bladed knife, make a vertical cut parallel to the long edge of the cake 11.5cm (4½in) in from one side. Next, make an additional cut parallel to the short edge so that the table cake has a length of 15cm (6in); the width will be 11.5cm (4½in) – see the carving sketch (**B**).

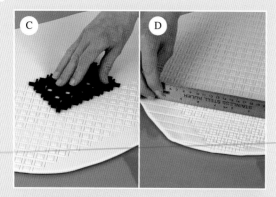

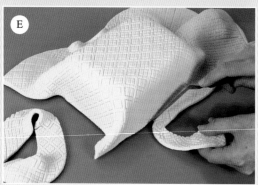

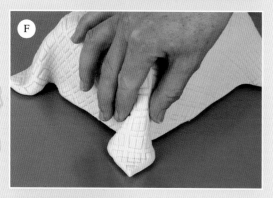

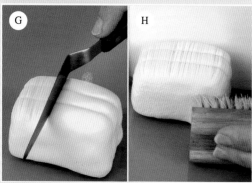

2 Using a small-bladed knife, round all the top edges of the table cake. For the bales, cut the remaining cake to a height of 4cm (1½in), discarding the excess, and then cut into five 6cm (2⅜in) long, 3.5cm (1⅜in) wide sections. Curve the top edges as for the table cake.

Covering the cake

1 Place the table cake on waxed paper and spread a thin layer of buttercream over to help stick the sugarpaste. Roll out 600g (1lb 5oz) of cream sugarpaste then take the trellis embosser or similar and repeatedly emboss the pattern onto the sugarpaste, making sure that the pattern is lined up correctly each time so that the overall pattern is seamless (**C**). Take a straightedge and emboss lines diagonally through the squares of the pattern to reduce the scale of the overall pattern (**D**).

2 Carefully pick up the paste, place it over the table cake and gently encourage the sides of the tablecloth in place leaving the pleats at the corners. Take a palette knife and cut away the excess paste at the base of the table by cutting a straight line from one side of the paste to the other, using the pattern on the sugarpaste as a guide (**E**). Position and smooth the pleats so that they look realistic (**F**) and then, if necessary, trim them to shape. Place to one side to dry.

Bales

1 To make the bales, place one bale cake onto waxed paper and cover with a thin layer of buttercream. Roll out 100g (3½oz) cream sugarpaste and use to cover the cake. Next, take the smoother and, with the flat edge at the base, run it along one side of the bale, pressing down into the excess paste at the same time to create a cutting line in the sugarpaste. Repeat for the other sides. Cut away the excess paste from the base using a palette knife.

2 Take the Dresden tool and, using the sharper, veining end, indent two parallel lines along the length of the bale to represent the baler twine. Next, take the palette knife and repeatedly indent lines at right angles to the twine (**G**). Then place the smoother on one long side of the bale and indent the other long side with a kitchen brush (**H**). Finally, define the edges of the long sides with some additional indents made with the pointed end of the Dresden tool. Repeat the sequence for the remaining bales.

Painting the bales

Dilute some of the golden-brown paste colour in clear spirit then paint over each of the bales allowing the paint to sink into the indentations and bring the bales to life. Set to one side to dry (**I**).

Stage Two

Carefully transfer the table cake to the covered board, placing it centrally. Arrange the dried bales around the table cake so that there are two along each side and one at the top.

The pigs

1 Pigs come in a variety of colours, shapes and sizes. The pigs in this project are made all the same size and shape but their colours/breeds are varied. Feel free to adapt yours as you wish. The instructions below are for one pig, so you will need to repeat them to make the number of pigs that you require.

Try looking on the Internet under pig breeds for ideas.

2 For the body, take 50g (2oz) of pig-coloured modelling paste, roll it into a ball and then elongate it slightly into a rounded sausage (**J**). Place the sausage upright on top of one of the bales, and then insert a piece of dried spaghetti through the top to support the head.

3 For the head, take 15g (½oz) of modelling paste and roll it into a 3cm (1⅛in) ball. Take the no. 4 piping tube and, using the larger end, indent a mouth by holding the tube at an angle to the ball (**K**). Indent the corners of the mouth using the smaller end of the tube, again holding it at an angle to the face. Next, open up the smile by using the wider end of the Dresden tool.

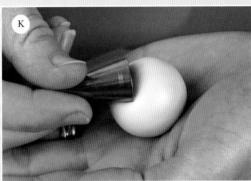

4 For the snout, roll a 1.3cm (½in) ball of modelling paste, flatten it slightly and attach it to the front of the face using sugar glue. Take a paintbrush and insert the end twice into the snout to form nostrils (**L**).

5 For the eyes, use a cocktail stick to indent two eyes above the snout. Then roll two small balls of black modelling paste and glue them in place with sugar glue.

To achieve small balls of paste, roll a small ball and cut in half, re-roll and cut in half again. Continue until you have two balls of the appropriate size.

6 For the ears, place the head on top of the body, then roll two pea-sized balls of paste. Pinch one end of each to flatten and widen it and pinch the other to a point (see picture J). Attach the wider end of each ear in position on top of the head using sugar glue.

7 For the hind legs, roll a 2.5cm (1in) ball of modelling paste and cut it into quarters. Take two quarters to make the hind legs. Roll each quarter into a ball and shape as for the ears (see picture J). Attach in place on the side of the body.

8 For the forelegs, roll the remaining quarters into balls. Elongate one side into a thin sausage, as shown (**M**). Next, take a small pair of scissors and remove a triangle from the end of the sausage to create the trotter. Repeat for the second foreleg. Attach in position on the cake, adjusting the position of each pig to help create an interesting tableaux.

9 For the tail, roll a small ball of modelling paste into a sausage, twirl it and place it onto the pig's behind.

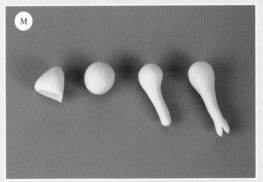

Making the plates and food

1 For the plates, roll out some of the blue, green, red and white modelling pastes between the narrow spacers, and cut out a selection of 3.25cm (1¼in) and 2.4cm (³¹⁄₃₂in) circles. Place the circles onto the foam. Take the 2.4cm (³¹⁄₃₂in) circle cutter and press it firmly into the centre of each large circle so that the paste around the cutter rises and creates the rim of the plates. Repeat for the smaller plates, this time using the wider end of a piping tube (**N**). Place a small plate in front of each pig and then arrange the remaining plates in the centre of the table.

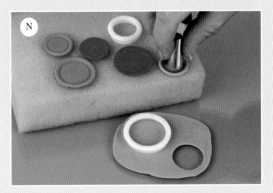

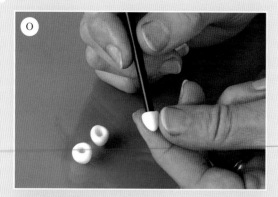

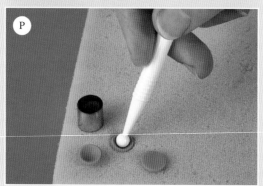

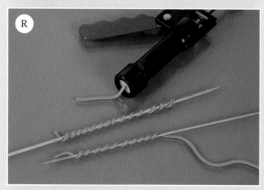

2 For the beakers, roll five pea-sized balls of modelling paste, then insert the handle of a paintbrush into each ball and mould the paste around it by gently squeezing the paste with your fingers (**O**). Place the resulting beakers on the table and, using a small paintbrush, fill with piping gel.

Colour the gel with paste colours to create different drinks.

3 For the jam tarts, colour some of the pig modelling- paste trimmings using the golden-brown paste colour. Roll out the modelling paste between the narrow spacers and cut out 1.3cm (½in) circles. Place the circles onto foam and press the small end of the ball tool into the centre of each to cup them (**P**). Roll small balls of red modelling paste and add to the centre of each tart. Add a small drop of piping gel on top of the red paste to add shine. Place a couple of tarts onto the pigs' plates and stack the remaining ones on a central plate.

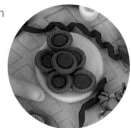

4 For the sandwiches, thickly roll out white and light brown modelling paste and cut out a number of 1cm (³⁄₈in) squares. Diagonally cut across each square and arrange the resulting triangle sandwiches on the plates.

5 For the crisps, add a touch of golden-brown paste colour to some of the light brown modelling paste and briefly mix so that the paste is marbled. Thinly roll out the paste and cut small circles using the nos 16 and 18 piping tubes. Place a circle in the palm of your hand and run the small end of the ball tool around the edges to slightly frill (**Q**). Repeat the sequence for the remaining circles and arrange on the plates.

6 For the carrots, take some of the orange modelling paste and roll it into small balls. Then roll each ball into a cone. Soften some of the green modelling paste. Do this by firstly kneading in some white vegetable fat to stop the paste becoming sticky and then partially dunking the paste into a small container of boiled water before kneading again (the paste should have the consistency of chewing gum). Place the softened paste with the small mesh disc into the sugar shaper. Squeeze out a little paste and remove a few strands with a Dresden tool. Stick the strands to the top of a carrot using sugar glue. Repeat for the other carrots. Arrange the carrots on the plates.

7 For the chocolate mini-rolls, roll a long, thin sausage of brown modelling paste and cut into short lengths to represent mini-rolls. Arrange on the plates.

The streamers

For the streamers, soften some of the red and orange modelling paste, as above, until it has the consistency of chewing gum. Place one of the softened pastes with the small ribbon disc into the sugar shaper. Squeeze out a length of paste then wrap it around a barbecue skewer. Repeat a number of times using both colours (**R**). Carefully slip off the coils of modelling paste and drape over the table and pigs.

Other decorations

1 For the balloons, roll a ball of modelling paste and then shape it into a cone. Thin a section of the pointed end between your fingers to represent the knot. Insert a cocktail stick into the end of the cone and circle it to enlarge the hole, then pinch around the edges to create the end of the balloon. Place on the covered board around the table. Make the strings by using softened black modelling paste and the sugar shaper fitted with the small mesh disc.

2 Create the party hats using different-coloured modelling pastes. Cut the crown-shaped hats from thinly rolled paste using a cutting wheel and then stick the two ends together to form a crown of the correct size. For the cone, roll a small ball of paste into a cone and decorate as desired. To make the pillbox hat, cut out a strip of paste and bring the ends together to form a small circle. Attach to the pig's head and decorate with small flowers or circles.

Finishing touches

To give the pigs a beady-eyed look, glaze the eyes using a paintbrush and confectioners' glaze. Add fillings to the sandwiches by painting thin lines in different colours along the cut edges of all the sandwiches. Using a non-toxic glue stick, attach the ribbon around the sides of the board to complete the cake.

Animal Magic

Personalize the pigs to represent party guests by dressing them in T-shirts with their initials on the front.

Go to town and dress the pigs up in party clothes as well.

For a large party, simply enlarge the table cake and increase the number of pigs.

Personalize the cake by using letter cutters to add a name, age and/or 'Happy Birthday' to the front of the board.

Cup Cakes

Cover the top of each cake with a disc of brown sugarpaste and texture it using a pan scourer as for the main cake. Model pigs' heads, as for the main cake, but cut the ball that forms the head in half so that it has a flat back and will sit neatly on top of the cup cake.

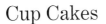

Templates

Increase all templates by 200%

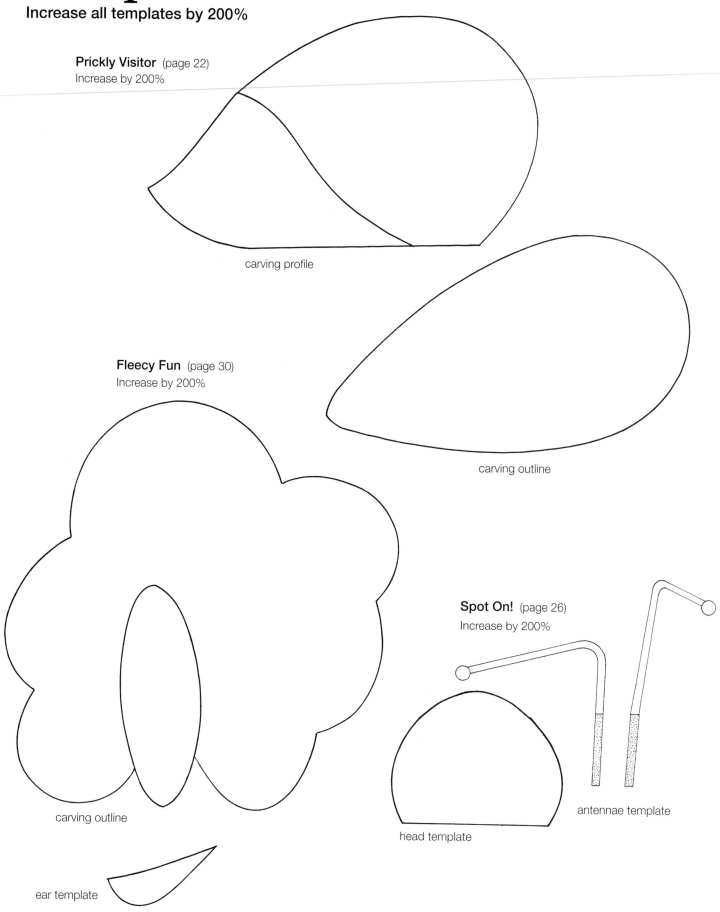

Prickly Visitor (page 22)
Increase by 200%

carving profile

Fleecy Fun (page 30)
Increase by 200%

carving outline

Spot On! (page 26)
Increase by 200%

carving outline

antennae template

head template

ear template

Increase all templates by 200%

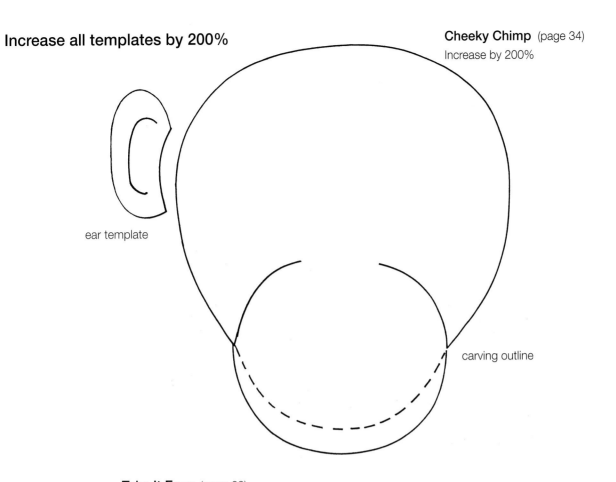

ear template

carving outline

Take It Easy (page 62)
Increase by 200%

Squeak with Delight (page 38)
Increase by 200%

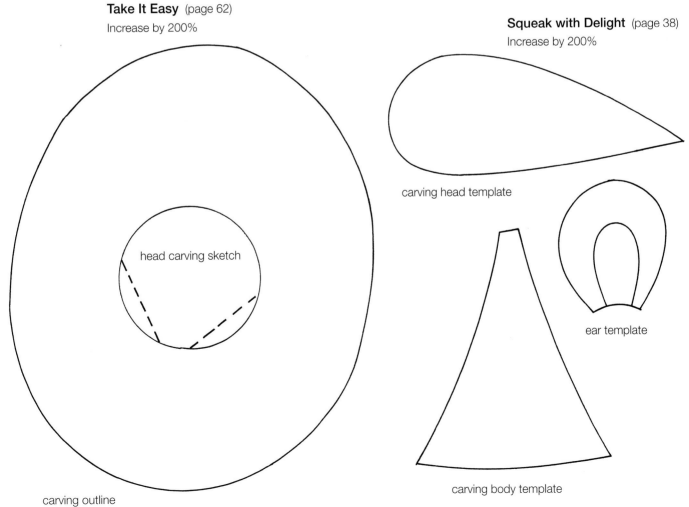

carving head template

head carving sketch

ear template

carving outline

carving body template

Increase all templates by 200%

Vamp It Up! (page 42)

Increase by 200%

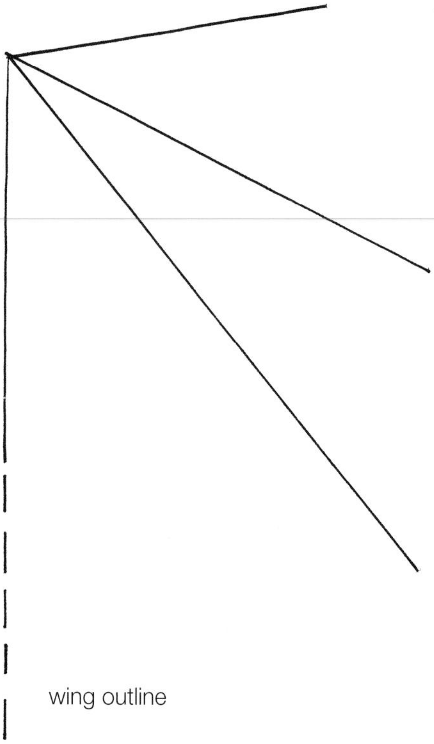

inner wing section

outer wing section

wing outline

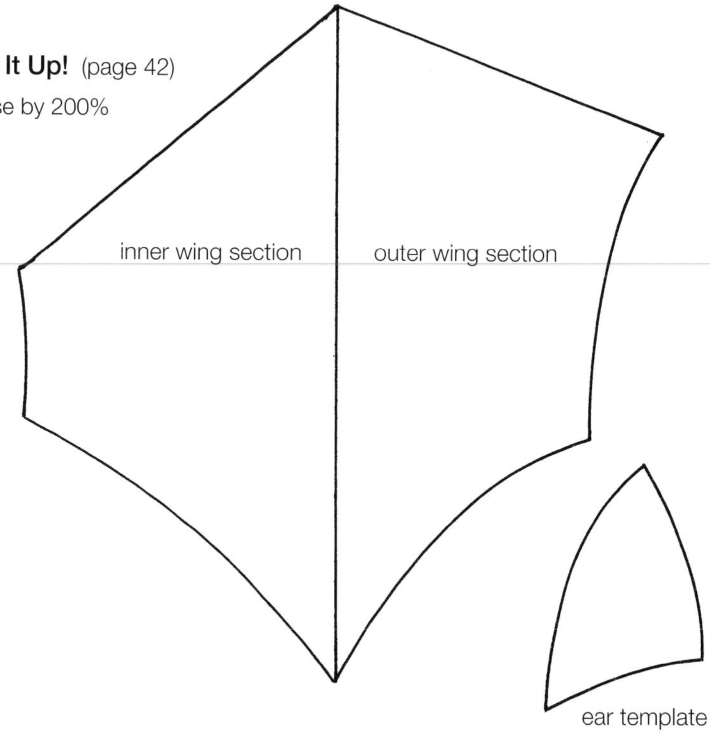

ear template

Whale of a Time (page 46)

Increase by 200%

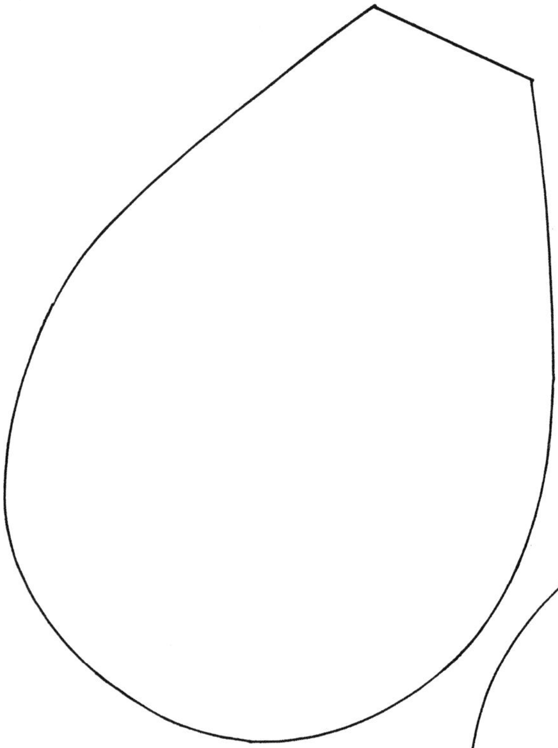

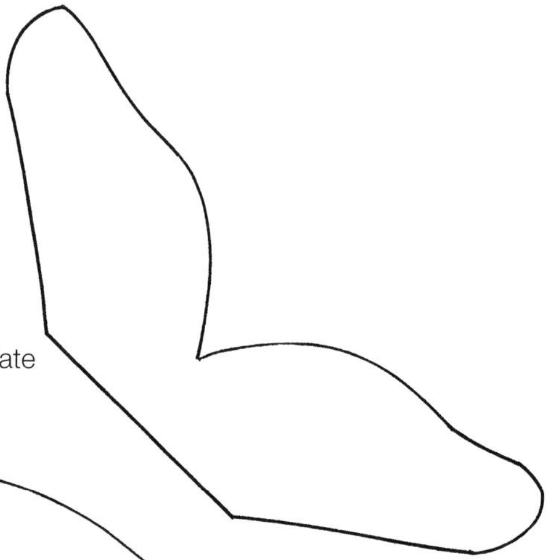

tail template

carving outline

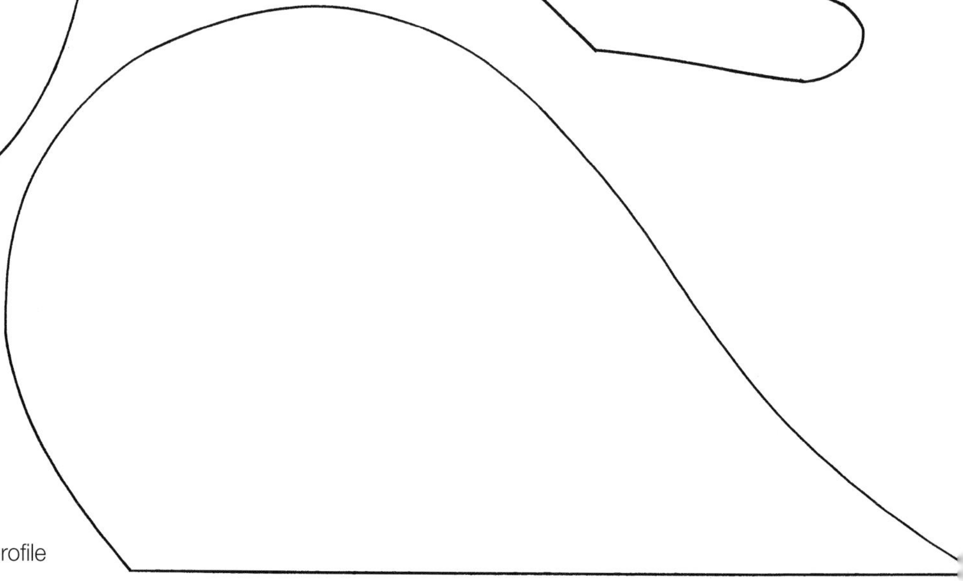

carving profile

Increase all templates by 200%

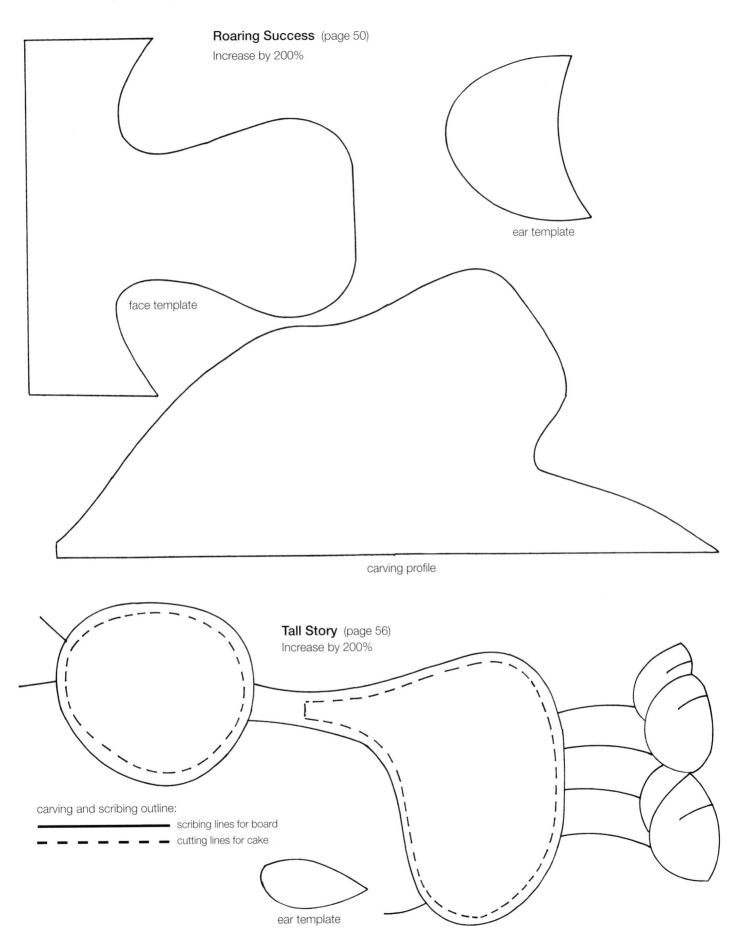

Roaring Success (page 50)
Increase by 200%

ear template

face template

carving profile

Tall Story (page 56)
Increase by 200%

carving and scribing outline:

———————— scribing lines for board
– – – – – – – cutting lines for cake

ear template

102

Increase all templates by 200%

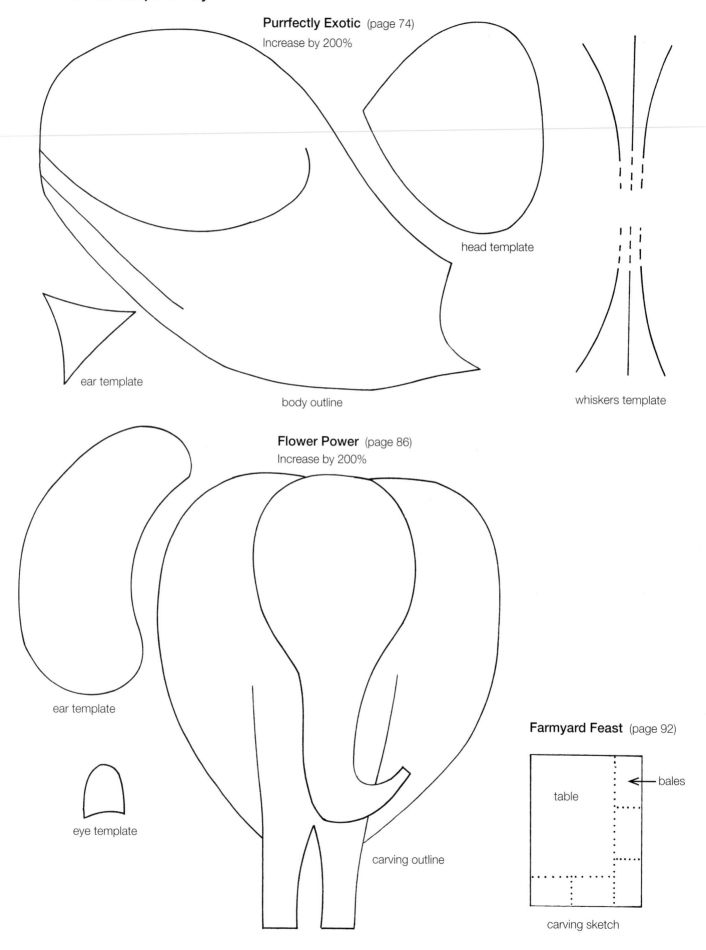

Purrfectly Exotic (page 74)
Increase by 200%

head template

ear template

body outline

whiskers template

Flower Power (page 86)
Increase by 200%

ear template

eye template

carving outline

Farmyard Feast (page 92)

table

bales

carving sketch

Increase all templates by 200%

Pool Party (page 68)
Increase by 200%

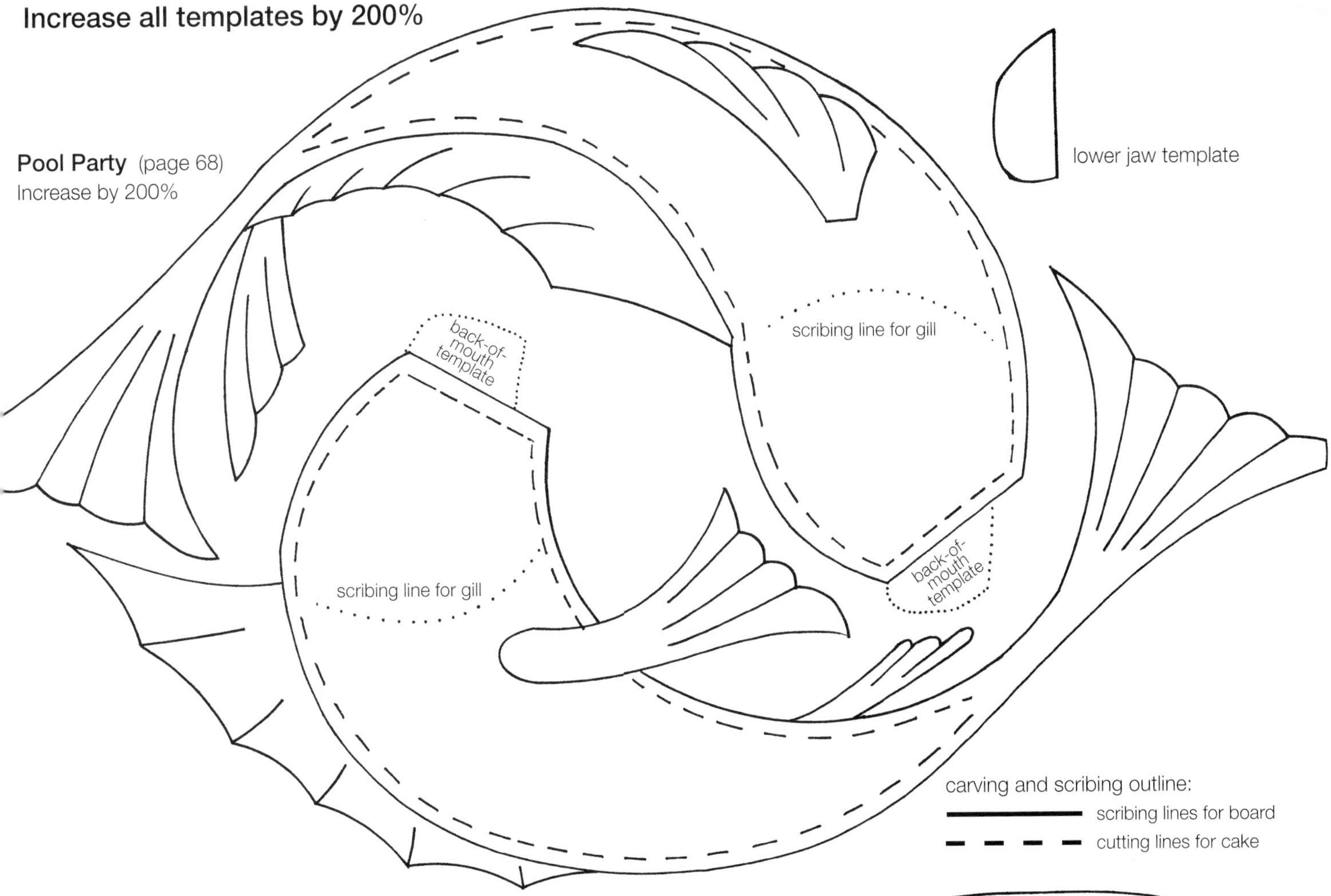

lower jaw template

back-of-mouth template

scribing line for gill

scribing line for gill

back-of-mouth template

carving and scribing outline:
scribing lines for board
cutting lines for cake

Top Dog (page 80)
Increase by 200%

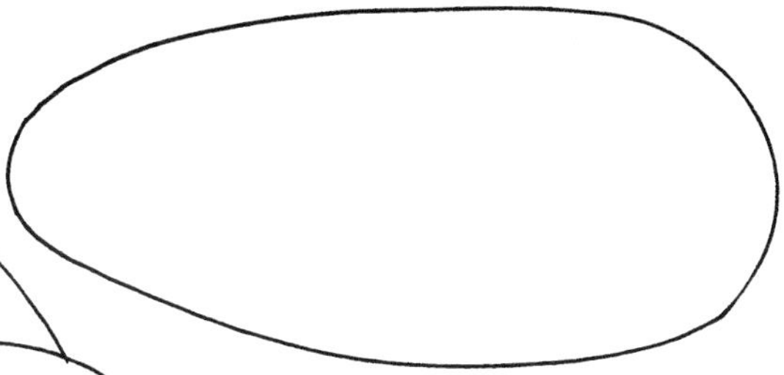

ear template

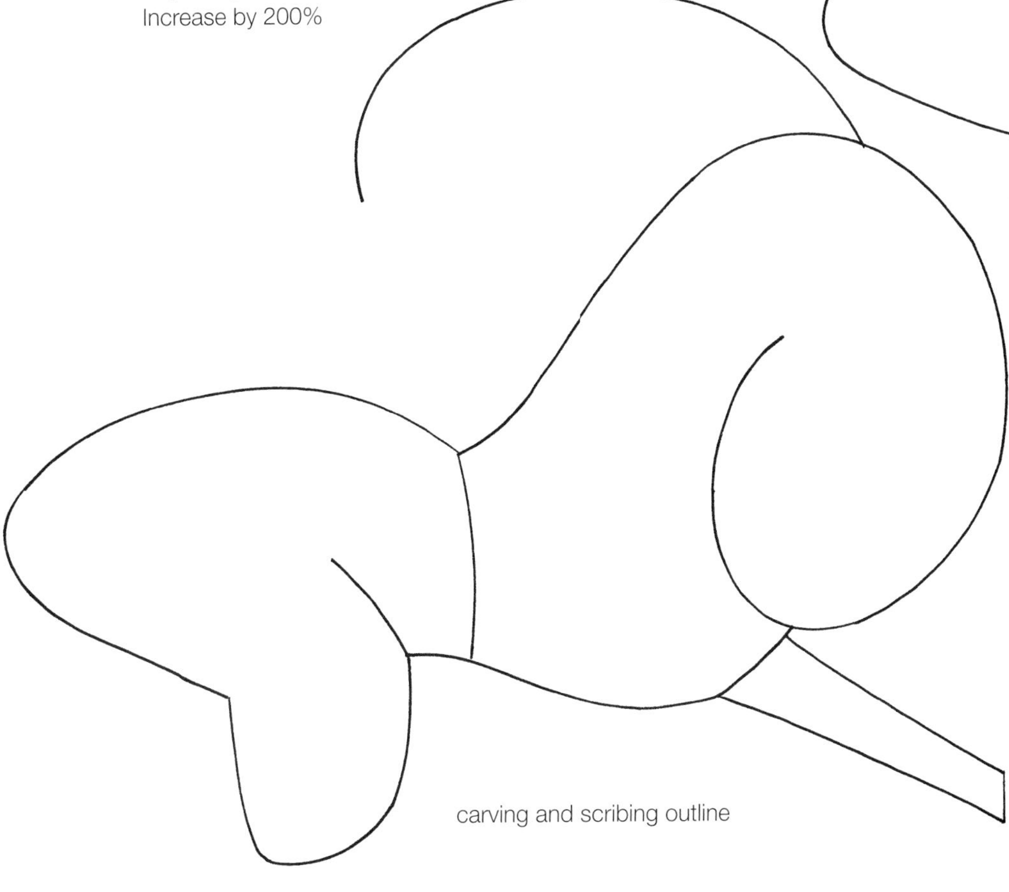

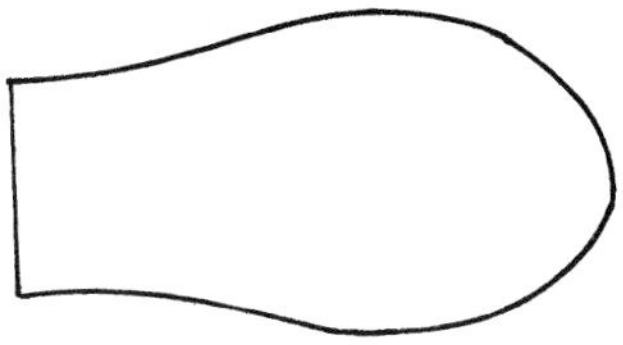

tongue template

carving and scribing outline

Acknowledgments

A special thank you goes to my family, especially my daughter Charlotte whose keen eye for detail, as always, was highly valued, and my sister Lucy, whose help with the cookies was greatly appreciated. Also a huge thank you to Jacqueline for baking the numerous cakes needed to complete the steps.

Thank you to M&B for supplying me with their superb range of sugarpaste – it has been great to use and saved me hours of colouring time.

I would also like to thank the team who have helped me put the book together: Karl whose photography has captured the character of the cakes – the tortoise is still my favourite; Jan, for being such a competent and reliable copy editor; Jenny, my editor, for all her help and innovative suggestions; and of course Lisa who created the look of the book.

About the author

Lindy Smith is a highly experienced cake designer and author of five other cake-decorating books. This is her fourth book for David & Charles, her first three being *Creative Celebration Cakes*, *Storybook Cakes* and *Celebrate with a Cake!*.

She began making novelty cakes when her children were small, and then, as the ideas began to flow, she created all kinds of special occasion cakes as commissions. Lindy now runs a highly successful cake design company called Lindy's Inspirational Cakes, which produces unusual and innovative, highly personalized wedding cakes. Her gorgeous creations, which are a world of imagination away from traditional wedding cakes, are frequently featured in wedding magazines, especially *Wedding Cakes – A Design Source*. Her personalized bride and groom cake toppers are especially popular with couples wishing to add that individual touch to their dream cake.

Lindy aims to improve the overall standard of novelty cakes and to bring the style of celebration cakes into the 21st century. She has appeared on television programmes such as *The Generation Game* and has also presented a sugarcraft series on *Good Food Live*. She is an accredited demonstrator of the British Sugarcraft Guild and her travels include Ireland, Scotland and New Zealand, where she always enjoys sharing her extensive knowledge with fellow sugarcrafters. Lindy's company also provides a mail-order service and on-line shop for sugarcraft equipment and cake separators, and her trade stand can usually be found at most of the major UK sugarcraft shows.

For more details please visit www.lindyscakes.co.uk.

Suppliers

UK

Alan Silverwood Ltd
Ledsam House
Ledsam Street
Birmingham B16 8DN
tel: +44(0)121 454 3571
email: sales@alan-silverwood.co.uk
manufacturer of multisized cake pan, multisized round and spherical moulds/ball tins (pans)

Ceefor Cakes
PO Box 443
Leighton Buzzard
Bedfordshire LU7 1AJ
tel: +44(0)1525 375237
email: ceefor.cakes@virgin.net
www.ceeforcakes.co.uk
supplier of strong cake boxes – most sizes available

FMM Sugarcraft (FMM)
Unit 5
Kings Park Industrial Estate
Primrose Hill
Kings Langley
Hertfordshire WD4 8ST
tel: +44 (0)1923 268699
email: clements@f-m-m.demon.co.uk
manufacturer of cutters

Knightsbridge PME Ltd (W)
Chadwell Heath Lane
Romford
Essex RN6 4NP
tel: +44 (0)20 859 05959
email: info@cakedecoration.co.uk
www.cakedecoration.co.uk
UK distributor of Wilton products

Lindy's Cakes Ltd (LC)
17 Grenville Avenue
Wendover
Bucks HP22 6AG
tel: +44(0)1296 623906
email: mailorder@lindyscakes.co.uk
www.lindyscakes.co.uk
mail-order supplier of much of the equipment used in this book

M&B Specialised Confectioners Ltd
3a Millmead Estate
Mill Mead Road
London N17 9ND
tel: +44(0)20 8801 7948
email: info@mbsc.co.uk
www.mbsc.co.uk
manufacturer and supplier of sugarpaste

Patchwork Cutters (PC)
3 Raines Close
Greasby, Wirral
Merseyside CH49 2QB
tel: +44 (0)151 6785053
supplier of cutters and embossers

A Piece of Cake
18–20 Upper High Street
Thame
Oxfordshire OX9 3EX
email: sales@sugaricing.com
www.sugaricing.com
shop and mail-order decorating supplies

US

Country Kitchen
4621 Speedway Drive
Fort Wayne
IN 46825
tel: +1 800 497 3927 or 260 482 4835
www.countrykitchensa.com

Sweet Celebrations Inc
PO Box 39426
Edina
MN 55439–0426
tel: +1 800 328 6722
www.sweetc.com

Wilton Industries, Inc. (W)
2240 West 75th Street
Woodridge
IL 60517
tel: +1 800 794 5866 (retail customer orders)
www.wilton.com

Australia

Cake Deco
Shop 7, Port Phillip Arcade
232 Flinders Street
Melbourne
Victoria
tel: (03)9654 5335
www.cakedeco.com.au
mail-order supplier

Iced Affair
53 Church Street
Camperdown
NSW 2050
tel: (02) 9519 3679
www.icedaffair.com
mail-order supplier

Abbreviations used in the book:

FMM	FMM Sugarcraft
LC	Lindy's Cakes Ltd
OP	Orchard Products
PC	Patchwork Cutters
PME	PME Sugarcraft
SK	Squire's Kitchen
W	Wilton

Index